THE GIVER

Lois Lowry

EDITORIAL DIRECTOR Justin Kestler
EXECUTIVE EDITOR Ben Florman
DIRECTOR OF TECHNOLOGY Tammy Hepps

SERIES EDITORS John Crowther, Justin Kestler
MANAGING EDITOR Vince Janoski

WRITER Caolan Madden
EDITOR John Crowther

SPARKNOTES is a registered trademark of SparkNotes LLC

This edition published by Spark Publishing

Spark Publishing
A Division of SparkNotes LLC
120 Fifth Avenue, 8th Floor
New York, NY 10011

Any book purchased without a cover is stolen property, reported as "unsold and
destroyed" to the Publisher, who receives no payment for such "stripped books."

Please submit all comments and questions or report errors to www.sparknotes.com/errors

Library of Congress Catalog-in-Publication Data available upon request

Printed and bound in the United States

ISBN 1-58663-816-5

Introduction:
Stopping to Buy
SparkNotes on a
Snowy Evening

Whose words these are you *think* you know.
Your paper's due tomorrow, though;
We're glad to see you stopping here
To get some help before you go.

Lost your course? You'll find it here.
Face tests and essays without fear.
Between the words, good grades at stake:
Get great results throughout the year.

Once school bells caused your heart to quake
As teachers circled each mistake.
Use SparkNotes and no longer weep,
Acc every single test you take.

Yes, books are lovely, dark, and deep,
But only what you grasp you keep,
With hours to go before you sleep,
With hours to go before you sleep.

Contents

CONTEXT   I

PLOT OVERVIEW   5

CHARACTER LIST   9

ANALYSIS OF MAJOR CHARACTERS   II
    JONAS   II
    THE GIVER   I2
    JONAS'S FATHER   I3

THEMES, MOTIFS & SYMBOLS   I5
    THE IMPORTANCE OF MEMORY   I5
    THE RELATIONSHIP BETWEEN PAIN AND PLEASURE   I5
    THE IMPORTANCE OF THE INDIVIDUAL   I6
    VISION   I6
    NAKEDNESS   I7
    RELEASE   I7
    THE NEWCHILD GABRIEL   I8
    THE SLED   I8
    THE RIVER   I8

SUMMARY & ANALYSIS   I9
    CHAPTERS 1–2   I9
    CHAPTERS 3–4   22
    CHAPTERS 5–6   25
    CHAPTERS 7–9   28
    CHAPTERS 10–11   32
    CHAPTERS 12–13   35
    CHAPTERS 14–16   39
    CHAPTERS 17–18   42
    CHAPTERS 19–20   46
    CHAPTERS 21–23   48

IMPORTANT QUOTATIONS EXPLAINED   53

KEY FACTS   59

STUDY QUESTIONS & ESSAY TOPICS   62
   STUDY QUESTIONS   62
   SUGGESTED ESSAY TOPICS   66

REVIEW & RESOURCES   68
   QUIZ   68
   SUGGESTIONS FOR FURTHER READING   74

CONTEXT

OIS LOWRY WAS BORN in 1937 in Honolulu, Hawaii. Because her father was in the army, Lowry moved around as a child. She lived in several different countries, including Japan. She attended Brown University, where she was a writing major, but left college before graduation to get married. Lowry's marriage did not last, but she had four children who became a major inspiration for her work. She finished her college degree at the University of Maine and worked as a housekeeper to earn a living. She continued to write, however, filled with ideas by the adventures of her children. In addition to working on young adult novels, Lowry also wrote textbooks and worked as a photographer specializing in children's portraits.

For her first novel, *A Summer to Die*, Lowry received the International Reading Association Children's Book Award in 1978. The novel tells the story of a thirteen-year-old girl's complex feelings toward her older sister, who is dying. Lowry has said that she does not like to include directly autobiographical information in her books, but it is possible that some of Lowry's experience seeped into *A Summer to Die*, as Lowry's own sister died of cancer.

Since then, Lowry has written more than twenty books for young adults, including the popular *Anastasia* series and *Number the Stars*, which won the Newbery Medal and the National Jewish Book Award in 1990. She was inspired to write *The Giver*—which won the 1994 Newbery medal—after visiting her elderly father in a nursing home. He had lost most of his long-term memory, and it occurred to Lowry that without memory there is no longer any pain. She imagined a society where the past was deliberately forgotten, which would allow the inhabitants to live in a kind of peaceful ignorance. The flaws inherent in such a society, she realized, would show the value of individual and community memory: although a loss of memory might mean a loss of pain, it also means a loss of lasting human relationships and connections with the past.

The society Lowry depicts in *The Giver* is a utopian society—a perfect world as envisioned by its creators. It has eliminated fear, pain, hunger, illness, conflict, and hatred—all things that most of us would like to eliminate in our own society. But in order to maintain the peace and order of their society, the citizens of the community in

The Giver have to submit to strict rules governing their behavior, their relationships, and even their language. Individual freedom and human passions add a chaotic element to society, and in *The Giver* even the memory of freedom and passion, along with the pain and conflict that human choice and emotion often cause, must be suppressed. In effect, the inhabitants of the society, though they are happy and peaceful, also lack the basic freedoms and pleasures that our own society values.

In this way, *The Giver* is part of the tradition of dystopian novels written in English, including George Orwell's *1984* and Aldous Huxley's *Brave New World*. In these novels, societies that might seem to be perfect because all the inhabitants are well fed or healthy or seemingly happy are revealed to be profoundly flawed because they limit the intellectual or emotional freedom of the individual. *1984* and *Brave New World* both feature characters who awaken to the richness of experience possible outside the confines of the society, but they are either destroyed by the society or reassimilated before they can make any significant changes. The books function as warnings to the reader: do not let this happen to your society.

The message of *The Giver* is slightly more optimistic: by the end of the novel, we believe that Jonas has taken a major step toward awakening his community to the rich possibilities of life. The novel is also slightly less realistic: although the technological advances that allow the community to function are scientifically feasible, the relationship between Jonas and the Giver has magical overtones. But Lowry's dystopian society shares many aspects with those of *1984* and *Brave New World*: the dissolution of close family connections and loyalty; the regulation or repression of sexuality; the regulation of careers, marriages, and reproduction; the subjugation of the individual to the community; and constant government monitoring of individual behavior.

The Giver was published in 1993, a time when public consciousness of political correctness was at a peak, and this historical context is interestingly echoed in some aspects of the society that Lowry portrays. One of the most prominent debates surrounding political correctness was—and is—the value of celebrating differences between people versus the value of making everyone in a society feel that they belong. The society in *The Giver*'s emphasis on "Sameness" can be seen as a critique of the politically correct tendency to ignore significant differences between individuals in order to avoid seeming prejudiced or discriminatory. At the same time, the society refuses to tolerate major differences between individuals at all: people who cannot be easily assimilated into the society are released. Lowry suggests that while tolerance is essential, it should never be achieved at the expense of true diversity.

In *The Giver*, Lowry tackles other issues that emerged as significant social questions in the early 1990s. The anti-abortion versus pro-life controversy raged hotly, and new questions arose concerning the ethics of a family's right to choose to end the life of a terminally ill family member (euthanasia) and an individual's right to end his or her own life (assisted suicide). Questions about reproductive rights and the nature of the family unit also arose due to advances in genetic and reproductive technology. Books such as Hillary Clinton's *It Takes a Village* and increased press coverage of single parents, extended families, gay parents, and community child-rearing raised complex questions about the forms families could take and the ways they could work.

Lowry's willingness to take on these issues in *The Giver*, as well as her insistence on treating all aspects of life in the community, has made *The Giver* one of the most frequently censored books in school libraries and curricula. Some parents are upset by the novel's depictions of sexuality and violence, and feel that their middle-school and high-school aged children are unprepared to deal with issues like euthanasia and suicide. Ironically, their desire to protect their children from these realities is not dissimilar to the novel's community's attempts to keep its citizens ignorant about—and safe from—sex, violence, and pain, both physical and psychological.

PLOT OVERVIEW

THE GIVER is written from the point of view of Jonas, an eleven-year-old boy living in a futuristic society that has eliminated all pain, fear, war, and hatred. There is no prejudice, since everyone looks and acts basically the same, and there is very little competition. Everyone is unfailingly polite. The society has also eliminated choice: at age twelve every member of the community is assigned a job based on his or her abilities and interests. Citizens can apply for and be assigned compatible spouses, and each couple is assigned exactly two children each. The children are born to Birthmothers, who never see them, and spend their first year in a Nurturing Center with other babies, or "newchildren," born that year. When their children are grown, family units dissolve and adults live together with Childless Adults until they are too old to function in the society. Then they spend their last years being cared for in the House of the Old until they are finally "released" from the society. In the community, release is death, but it is never described that way; most people think that after release, flawed newchildren and joyful elderly people are welcomed into the vast expanse of Elsewhere that surrounds the communities. Citizens who break rules or fail to adapt properly to the society's codes of behavior are also released, though in their cases it is an occasion of great shame. Everything is planned and organized so that life is as convenient and pleasant as possible.

Jonas lives with his father, a Nurturer of new children, his mother, who works at the Department of Justice, and his seven-year-old sister Lily. At the beginning of the novel, he is apprehensive about the upcoming Ceremony of Twelve, when he will be given his official Assignment as a new adult member of the community. He does not have a distinct career preference, although he enjoys volunteering at a variety of different jobs. Though he is a well-behaved citizen and a good student, Jonas is different: he has pale eyes, while most people in his community have dark eyes, and he has unusual powers of perception. Sometimes objects "change" when he looks at them. He does not know it yet, but he alone in his community can perceive flashes of color; for everyone else, the world is as devoid of color as it is of pain, hunger, and inconvenience.

At the Ceremony of Twelve, Jonas is given the highly honored Assignment of Receiver of Memory. The Receiver is the sole keeper of the community's collective memory. When the community went over to Sameness—its painless, warless, and mostly emotionless state of tranquility and harmony—it abandoned all memories of pain, war, and emotion, but the memories cannot disappear totally. Someone must keep them so that the community can avoid making the mistakes of the past, even though no one but the Receiver can bear the pain. Jonas receives the memories of the past, good and bad, from the current Receiver, a wise old man who tells Jonas to call him the Giver.

The Giver transmits memories by placing his hands on Jonas's bare back. The first memory he receives is of an exhilarating sled ride. As Jonas receives memories from the Giver—memories of pleasure and pain, of bright colors and extreme cold and warm sun, of excitement and terror and hunger and love—he realizes how bland and empty life in his community really is. The memories make Jonas's life richer and more meaningful, and he wishes that he could give that richness and meaning to the people he loves. But in exchange for their peaceful existence, the people of Jonas's community have lost the capacity to love him back or to feel deep passion about anything. Since they have never experienced real suffering, they also cannot appreciate the real joy of life, and the life of individual people seems less precious to them. In addition, no one in Jonas's community has ever made a choice of his or her own. Jonas grows more and more frustrated with the members of his community, and the Giver, who has felt the same way for many years, encourages him. The two grow very close, like a grandfather and a grandchild might have in the days before Sameness, when family members stayed in contact long after their children were grown.

Meanwhile, Jonas is helping his family take care of a problem newchild, Gabriel, who has trouble sleeping through the night at the Nurturing Center. Jonas helps the child to sleep by transmitting soothing memories to him every night, and he begins to develop a relationship with Gabriel that mirrors the family relationships he has experienced through the memories. When Gabriel is in danger of being released, the Giver reveals to Jonas that release is the same as death. Jonas's rage and horror at this revelation inspire the Giver to help Jonas devise a plan to change things in the community forever. The Giver tells Jonas about the girl who had been designated the new Receiver ten years before. She had been the Giver's own daughter, but the sadness of some of the memories had been too much for her and she had asked to be released. When she died, all of the memories she had accumulated were released into the community, and the community member[s] [co]uld not handle the sudden influx of emotion and [se...] [...]er and Jonas plan for Jonas to escape th[...] enter Elsewhere. Once he [...] ries will disperse, and the [...] terms with the new feel[...]ever.

[...] than planned when his [...] the next day. Desperate [...]le and a supply of food [...]ers a landscape full of [...] hunger, danger, and [...] Gabriel travel for a [...]mpossible. Half-fro-[...] unshine and friend-[...]led—the sled from [...] the top. Jonas and [...] he sled. Ahead of [...] ghts of a friendly [...] sure that some-

o Radios, stereo equipments
o Vacuum cleaners
o Video games and consoles
o Wiring and cables

The Exchange Zone (materials must condition and reusable)
•
o Art and office supplies
o Bicycles and parts
o Corks
o Garden pots
o Hangers- metal, plastic, or wood hangers
o Media- books, magazines, DVD: tapes, video tapes
o Reading Glasses- Lion's Club exchange located next to book exchange
o Packaging materials
o Sporting goods

PLOT OVERVIEW

CHARACTER LIST

Jonas   The eleven-year-old protagonist of *The Giver*. Sensitive and intelligent, with strange powers of perception that he doesn't understand, Jonas is chosen to be the new Receiver of Memory for his community when he turns twelve. Even before his training, Jonas is unusually thoughtful, expresses great concern for his friends and family, and thinks it would be nice to be closer to other people. After his training begins, Jonas's universe widens dramatically. His new awareness of strong emotions, beautiful colors, and great suffering makes him extremely passionate about the world around him and the welfare of the people he loves, though on the whole he remains level-headed and thoughtful.

The Giver   The old man known in the community as the Receiver of Memory. The Giver has held the community's collective memory for many years and uses his wisdom to help the Committee of Elders make important decisions, even though he is racked by the pain his memories give him and believes that perhaps those memories belong in the minds of everyone in the community.

Jonas's father   A mild-mannered, tenderhearted Nurturer who works with infants. He is very sweet with his two children. He enjoys his job and takes it very seriously, constantly trying to nurture children who will stay alive until the Ceremony of Names. However, even if he is attached to a child, he will release it if that seems to be the best decision. He has an affectionate, playful relationship with his two children, usually referring to them by silly nicknames, and he likes playing childish games with the children he nurtures.

Jonas's mother A practical, pleasant woman with an important position at the Department of Justice. Jonas's mother takes her work seriously, hoping to help people who break rules see the error of their ways. She frequently gives Jonas advice about the worries and fears he faces as he grows up.

Lily Jonas's seven-year-old sister. She is a chatterbox and does not know quite when to keep her mouth shut, but she is also extremely practical and well-informed for a little girl.

Gabriel The newchild that Jonas's family cares for at night. He is sweet and adorable during the day, but has trouble sleeping at night unless Jonas puts him to sleep with some memories. He and Jonas become very close.

Asher Jonas's best friend. Asher is a fun-loving, hasty boy who usually speaks too fast, mixing up his words to the exasperation of his teachers and Jonas. He is assigned the position of Assistant Director of Recreation.

Fiona Another of Jonas's friends. She has red hair, which only Jonas can see, and works as a Caretaker in the House of the Old. She is mild-mannered and patient. Jonas's first sexual stirrings come in the form of an erotic dream about Fiona.

Larissa A woman living in the House of the Old. Jonas shares pleasant conversation with her while he gives her a bath during his volunteer hours. Like many inhabitants of the House of the Old, she enjoys gossip and looks forward to her release.

The Chief Elder The elected leader of Jonas's community. She to shows genuine affection for all of the children at the Ceremony of Twelve, knowing of their names and an anecdote about each one.

Analysis of Major Characters

Jonas

On the surface, Jonas is like any other eleven-year-old boy living in his community. He seems more intelligent and perceptive than many of his peers, and he thinks more seriously than they do about life, worrying about his own future as well as his friend Asher's. He enjoys learning and experiencing new things: he chooses to volunteer at a variety of different centers rather than focusing on one, because he enjoys the freedom of choice that volunteer hours provide. He also enjoys learning about and connecting with other people, and he craves more warmth and human contact than his society permits or encourages. The things that really set him apart from his peers—his unusual eyes, his ability to see things change in a way that he cannot explain—trouble him, but he does not let them bother him too much, since the community's emphasis on politeness makes it easy for Jonas to conceal or ignore these little differences. Like any child in the community, Jonas is uncomfortable with the attention he receives when he is singled out as the new Receiver, preferring to blend in with his friends.

Once Jonas begins his training with the Giver, however, the tendencies he showed in his earlier life—his sensitivity, his heightened perceptual powers, his kindness to and interest in people, his curiosity about new experiences, his honesty, and his high intelligence—make him extremely absorbed in the memories the Giver has to transmit. In turn, the memories, with their rich sensory and emotional experiences, enhance all of Jonas's unusual qualities. Within a year of training, he becomes extremely sensitive to beauty, pleasure, and suffering, deeply loving toward his family and the Giver, and fiercely passionate about his new beliefs and feelings. Things about the community that used to be mildly perplexing or troubling are now intensely frustrating or depressing, and Jonas's inherent concern for others and desire for justice makes him yearn to make changes in the community, both to awaken other people to the richness of life and to stop the casual cruelty that is practiced in the community. Jonas is also very determined, committing to a task fully when he believes in it and willing to risk his own life for the sake of the people he loves.

Although as a result of his training Jonas possesses more wisdom than almost anyone else in his community, he is still very young and knows little about life in the community itself. At twelve years old, Jonas is too young to control the powerful emotions that his training unleashes, and the natural hormonal imbalances of preadolesnce make him especially passionate and occasionally unreasonable. Of course, his youth makes it possible for him to receive the memories and learn from them—if he were older, he might be less receptive to new experiences and emotions—but he needs the guidance and wisdom of the Giver, who has life experience as well as memories, to help him keep all of his new experiences in perspective.

THE GIVER

Like Jonas, who is a young person with the wisdom of an old person, the Giver is a bit of a paradox. He looks ancient, but he is not old at all. Like someone who has seen and done many things over many years, he is very wise and world-weary, and he is haunted by memories of suffering and pain, but in reality his life has been surprisingly uneventful. In the world of the community, the Giver has spent most of his life inside his comfortable living quarters, eating his meals and emerging occasionally to take long walks. Yet he carries the memories of an entire community, so he feels like a man who has done more in his life than anyone else in the world: he has experienced the positive and negative emotions, desires, triumphs, and failures of millions of men and women, as well as animals. He is responsible for preserving those memories and using the wisdom they give him to make decisions for the community. Anyone would feel weighted down by this enormous responsibility, and because the Giver is forbidden to share his knowledge and pain with anyone else, including his spouse and his children, the weight is more difficult to bear. Thus, the Giver has become an exceptionally patient, quiet, deliberate person, growing resigned to the fact that he cannot change the community even though he realizes that it needs to be changed. He endures his loneliness and frustration as well as the increasing physical pain that the memories bring him with a quiet calm that makes him a rather stoic figure. His patience, wisdom, and restraint make him an excellent teacher and mentor.

However, the memories that the Giver carries inside him are too powerful for him to be entirely stoic: he still feels strong emotions, and under the right circumstances they surge to the surface. Among the members of the community, the Giver alone is capable of real love, an emotion he experiences with Rosemary, the first child who was designated to be the Receiver. Years of loneliness, isolation, and unshared emotion made the Giver's love for Rosemary intense, even by the standards of the time before Sameness, and when she is taken from him, his anger and grief are equally intense. It is this anger and grief, fueled by the Giver's growing love for Jonas and Jonas's own youthful energy, that allow the Giver to finally overturn his years of silence and endurance and change the community. The decision is also influenced by the Giver's aptitude as a teacher and advisor: it is natural for him to want to help the community learn to handle the memories, as he has helped Rosemary and Jonas.

JONAS'S FATHER

Jonas's father is one of the only characters in the novel, besides the Giver and Jonas, who seems to grapple with difficult decisions and complex emotions. Although Jonas's father does not have access to the memories that give Jonas and the Giver insight into human relationships and feelings, he displays many of the characteristics that were valued in pre-Sameness societies. As a Nurturer, he feels a strong connection with the babies he cares for and a deep concern for their welfare. Although he agrees with Jonas's mother that "love" is a meaningless, obscure word, the feelings he displays toward the newchildren and his family seem very much like love: he delights in taking care of them and playing with them, he worries about them, and he makes minor and major sacrifices for their benefit, from indulging his daughter's fondness for her comfort object to bringing baby Gabriel home to his family every night in the hopes of saving him from being released. His concern for the newchildren might be concern about his own personal failure as a Nurturer, but he obviously feels pain and regret when children are released. He also has an independent streak that is unusual in the community, demonstrated when he breaks a rule and peeks at Gabriel's name in the hopes that it will help the child.

In the end, however, Jonas's father is a product of his society. Under other circumstances, he probably would have loved the new-children passionately and fought against all odds for their survival. But having grown up in a society where release, though an occasion for sadness, is not considered tragedy, Jonas's father cannot access the deeper feelings that might be available to him. He regrets the release of newchildren, but he performs releases himself: not knowing the value of life as Jonas does, he cannot appreciate its loss, and never having felt intense pain, he cannot summon it for the death of a baby.

THEMES, MOTIFS & SYMBOLS

THEMES

Themes are the fundamental and often universal ideas explored in a literary work.

THE IMPORTANCE OF MEMORY

One of the most important themes in *The Giver* is the significance of memory to human life. Lowry was inspired to write *The Giver* after a visit to her aging father, who had lost most of his long-term memory. She realized that without memory, there is no pain—if you cannot remember physical pain, you might as well not have experienced it, and you cannot be plagued by regret or grief if you cannot remember the events that hurt you. At some point in the past the community in *The Giver* decided to eliminate all pain from their lives. To do so, they had to give up the memories of their society's collective experiences. Not only did this allow them to forget all of the pain that had been suffered throughout human history, it also prevented members of the society from wanting to engage in activities and relationships that could result in conflict and suffering, and eliminated any nostalgia for the things the community gave up in order to live in total peace and harmony. According to the novel, however, memory is essential. The Committee of Elders does recognize the practical applications of memory—if you do not remember your errors, you may repeat them—so it designates a Receiver to remember history for the community. But as Jonas undergoes his training, he learns that just as there is no pain without memory, there is also no true happiness.

THE RELATIONSHIP BETWEEN PAIN AND PLEASURE

Related to the theme of memory is the idea that there can be no pleasure without pain and no pain without pleasure. No matter how delightful an experience is, you cannot value the pleasure it gives you unless you have some memory of a time when you have suffered. The members of Jonas's community cannot appreciate the joys in their lives because they have never felt pain: their lives are totally monotonous, devoid of emotional variation. Similarly, they do not feel pain or grief because they do not appreciate the true wonder of life: death is not tragic to them because life is not precious. When Jonas receives memories from the Giver, the memories of pain open him to the idea of love and comfort as much as the memories of pleasure do.

THE IMPORTANCE OF THE INDIVIDUAL

At the Ceremony of Twelve, the community celebrates the differences between the twelve-year-old children for the first time in their lives. For many children, twelve is an age when they are struggling to carve out a distinct identity for themselves, differentiating themselves from their parents and peers. Among other things, *The Giver* is the story of Jonas's development into an individual, maturing from a child dependent upon his community into a young man with unique abilities, dreams, and desires. The novel can even be seen as an allegory for this process of maturation: twelve-year-old Jonas rejects a society where everyone is the same to follow his own path. The novel encourages readers to celebrate differences instead of disparaging them or pretending they do not exist. People in Jonas's society ignore his unusual eyes and strange abilities out of politeness, but those unusual qualities end up bringing lasting, positive change to the community.

MOTIFS

Motifs are recurring structures, contrasts, or literary devices that can help to develop and inform the text's major themes.

VISION

The motif of vision runs throughout *The Giver*, from the first mention of Jonas's unusual pale eyes to the final image of the lights twinkling in the village in Elsewhere. For most of the novel, vision represents all perception, both sensory and emotional. Jonas's eyes, which appear to be "deeper" than other people's, are actually able to see more deeply into objects than other people's eyes: Jonas is one of the few people in the community who can see color. Jonas's perception of color symbolizes his perception of the complicated emotions and sensations that other people cannot perceive: he sees life differently from the rest of the community. Jonas shares his abilities with the Giver and Gabe, both of whom have eyes the same color as his. Although the ending of the novel is ambiguous, we know that Jonas sees the village in his mind, even if the village does not really exist.

NAKEDNESS

In Jonas's community, it is forbidden to look at naked people, unless they are very young or very old. Moments involving physical nakedness are closely related to the idea of emotional nakedness: Jonas feels an emotional connection with the old woman, Larissa, when she trusts him to wash her body, and his training involves receiving memories through his bare back. Both situations involve trust and intimacy; both are curiously related to the idea of freedom. Jonas thinks of the naked woman as "free," perhaps because he associates her physical nudity with a mind bare of the constraints his society places on human behavior, and the information that the Giver transmits to him is liberating in much the same way—it helps him to look beyond the community's rules and beliefs. Nakedness is also related to innocence and childishness: the Old can be seen naked because they are treated like children, and Jonas's relationship to the Giver is like a child's to his father or grandfather.

RELEASE

Though few people know it, the word "release" actually refers to death—or murder—in Jonas's society, but throughout *The Giver*, the word means different things to different people. At the beginning of the novel, most of the characters truly believe that people who are released are physically sent to Elsewhere, the world beyond the limits of the community. Release is frightening or sad because no one would want to leave the community, not because it involves violence or death. Later, when Jonas discovers the real meaning of release, the word becomes ominous. At the end of the novel, however, when Jonas escapes despite the fact that he is forbidden to request release, he changes the meaning of the word once again, restoring its original meaning—an escape from the physical and psychological hold of the community.

MOTIFS

SYMBOLS

Symbols are objects, characters, figures, or colors used to represent abstract ideas or concepts.

THE NEWCHILD GABRIEL

For Jonas, the newchild Gabriel is a symbol of hope and of starting over. Babies frequently figure as symbols of hope and regeneration in literature, and in *The Giver* this makes perfect sense: Gabriel is too young to have absorbed the customs and rules of the community, so he is still receptive to the powerful memories that Jonas transmits to him. Jonas takes Gabriel with him to save Gabriel's life, but his gesture is also symbolic of his resolve to change things, to start a new life Elsewhere. His struggles to keep Gabriel alive reflect his struggles to maintain his ideals in the face of difficulty.

THE SLED

The sled, the first memory Jonas receives from the Giver, symbolizes the journey Jonas takes during his training and the discoveries he makes. It is red, a color that symbolizes the new, vital world of feelings and ideas that Jonas discovers. Before he transmits the memory, the Giver compares the difficulty he has in carrying the memories to the way a sled slows down as snow accumulates on its runners. The novelty and delight of the downhill ride are exhilarating, and Jonas enjoys the ride in the same way that he enjoys accumulating new memories. But the sled can be treacherous, too: the first memory of extreme pain that he experiences involves the sled. Pleasure and pain are inevitably related on the sled, just as they are in the memories. When, at the end of the novel, Jonas finds a real sled, it symbolizes his entry into a world where color, sensation, and emotion exist in reality, not just in memory.

THE RIVER

The river, which runs into the community and out of it to Elsewhere, symbolizes escape from the confines of the community. When little Caleb drowns in the river, it is one of the few events that the community cannot predict or control, and Jonas and the Giver are inspired to try to change the community by the idea of the river's unpredictable behavior.

SUMMARY & ANALYSIS

CHAPTERS 1–2

SUMMARY

We are introduced to Jonas, the eleven-year-old protagonist of the story, as he struggles to find the right word to describe his feelings as he approaches an important milestone. He rejects "frightened" as too strong a word, recalling a time when he had really been frightened: a year ago, an unidentified aircraft flew over his community—it was a strange and unprecedented event, since Pilots were not allowed to fly over the community. As Jonas remembers the community reaction to the event, we learn more about the society in which he lives. It is extremely structured, with official orders transmitted through loudspeakers planted all around the community. As a punishment, the pilot was "released" from the community—the worst fate that can befall a citizen. Jonas decides he is apprehensive, not frightened, about the important thing that is going to happen in December. Jonas and his society value the use of precise and accurate language.

At dinner that night, Jonas's family—his father, mother, and seven-year-old sister Lily—participate in a nightly ritual called "the telling of feelings." Each person describes an emotion that he or she experienced during the day and discusses it with the others. Lily says she was angry at a child visiting from a nearby community who did not observe her childcare group's play area rules. Her parents help her to understand that the boy probably felt out of place, and she becomes less angry. Jonas's father, who is a Nurturer (he takes care of the community's babies, or newchildren), describes his struggles with a slowly developing baby whose weakness makes it a candidate for release. The family considers taking care of the baby for a while, though they are not allowed to adopt him—every household is allowed only one male and one female child. We also learn that spouses are assigned by the government. Jonas explains his apprehensiveness about the coming Ceremony of Twelve—the time when he will be assigned a career and begin life as an adult. We learn that every December, all of the children in the community are promoted to the next age group—all four-year-old children become Fives, regardless of the time of year when they were actually born. We also learn that fifty children are born every year. The ceremonies are different for each age group. At the Ceremony of One newchildren, who have spent their first year at the Nurturing Center, are assigned to family units and given a name to use in addition to the number they were given at birth. Jonas's father confesses to his family that he has peeked at the struggling newchild's name—Gabriel—in the hopes that calling him a name will help the child develop more quickly. Jonas is surprised that his father would break any kind of rule, though the members of the community seem to bend rules once in a while. For instance, older siblings often teach younger siblings to ride bicycles before the Ceremony of Nine, when they receive their first official bicycles.

Jonas's parents reassure him that the Committee of Elders, the ruling group of the community, will choose a career for him that will suit him. The Committee members observe the Elevens all year, at school and play and at the volunteer work they are required to do after school, and consider each child's abilities and interests when they make their selection. Jonas's father tells him that when he was eleven, he knew he would be assigned the role of Nurturer, because it was clear that he loved newchildren and he spent all his volunteer hours in the Nurturing Center. When Jonas expresses concern about his friend Asher's Assignment—he worries that Asher does not have any serious interests—his parents tell him not to worry, but remind him that after Twelve, he might lose touch with many of his childhood friends, since he will be spending his time with a new group, training for his job. Then Jonas's sister Lily appears, asking for her "comfort object"—a community-issued stuffed elephant. The narrator refers to the comfort objects as "imaginary creatures. Jonas's had been called a bear."

ANALYSIS

At the beginning of *The Giver*, we have a difficult time figuring out the setting of the novel. We do not know what it is that Jonas is afraid of—from the reference to unidentified aircraft, we might think that he lives in a war zone. When we find out that it is against the rules for Pilots to fly over the community, we know that Jonas lives in a community that is different from our own, but we do not know at first how different it. Lowry allows the small details about life in Jonas's community to build up gradually into a more complete picture.

Initially, the picture we get of Jonas's society is positive. From the emphasis on precision of language and the considerate, careful way in which Jonas's family shares its feelings, we learn that his society values the clear communication of ideas. We also know that members of the community pay attention to each other's feelings and try to solve each other's problems in rational, reassuring ways: the family helps Lily to control her anger and encourages her to feel empathy for visitors in unfamiliar surroundings, and they resolve to help their father take care of a struggling baby. The community must be very safe and peaceful indeed if the only time Jonas can remember being frightened is when an unidentified plane flew over his community.

Some aspects of life in the community are startling, but they are easily explained. The loudspeakers transmitting orders to the people in the community are somewhat unsettling—the idea of a disembodied, faceless authority with the power to control many people's actions is reminiscent of police states and dictatorships. At the same time, it is a convenient public address system that was able to reassure many frightened people. The fact that the government chooses people's spouses, jobs, and children for them is also unsettling, but the picture we get of Jonas's family life is full of tranquility and comfort—the system obviously works pretty well. We know that the society is extremely orderly and peaceful, and that everyone has a job that he or she enjoys and can do well. There seems to be very little competition in Jonas's community. Jonas is not hoping for a desirable or prestigious position, just one that he will be able to do well. In general, the society seems to be an almost perfect model of a communist society, one in which everyone in the community works together for the common good and receives an equal share of the benefits of living in the community.

However, the discordant notes remain, highlighted by Jonas's description of himself as "frightened" at the beginning of the book. Even though he immediately rejects the word as inaccurate, its appearance in the first sentence of the novel colors the mood of the first several pages. Since Jonas seems so comfortable with the more unusual aspects of his society, we begin to think of them as normal, but at the same time his fear at the beginning of the story makes us slightly wary of totally accepting them. We are more likely now to notice that the society's rules, though they are meant to help its citizens, limit personal freedom. We are also more likely to pick up on the ominous meaning of release—the punishment given to the pilot who accidentally flew over the community. Why would an accident be given the most serious punishment in the community? What does release actually mean? The word usually has a positive meaning, but in this context it is negative. In the tension between the two meanings, Lowry hints that everything in the society might not be exactly how it seems.

By the end of Chapter 1, though Jonas has decided he is not frightened, he has decided that he is apprehensive. Having accepted that Jonas likes living in his community with his family, we have grown less frightened and more apprehensive with him. However, we have the feeling that, just like Jonas, the entire novel is on the brink of an important change. Jonas's apprehension is a kind of foreshadowing that gets us ready for the idea that the whole society he lives in might be reaching an important milestone very soon, just as Jonas awaits the important milestone of the Ceremony of Twelve.

CHAPTERS 3–4

SUMMARY

> *He liked the feeling of safety here in this warm and quiet*
> *room; he liked the expression of trust on the woman's*
> *face as she lay in the water unprotected, exposed,*
> *and free.*   (See QUOTATIONS, p. 53)

Jonas's father brings the struggling newchild Gabriel home to spend nights with Jonas's family. Lily remarks that Gabriel has "funny eyes" like Jonas—both boys have light eyes, while most people in the community have darker eyes. Lily is being slightly rude: in their society it is inappropriate to call attention to the ways in which people are different. Lily also says she hopes she will be assigned to be a Birthmother when she grows up, since she likes newchildren so much, but her mother tells her that the position of Birthmother carries very little honor—Birthmothers are pampered for three years while they produce children, but then do hard labor and never get to see their biological children.

Jonas thinks about the Speakers who make announcements to the community over the loudspeakers all day, including reprimands to rule-breakers. He remembers a time when an announcement was specifically directed at him, though his name was not mentioned—no one is singled out in his society. The announcement reminded male Elevens that "snacks are to be eaten, not hoarded," referring to an apple that he had taken home with him from school. Jonas had taken the apple because, while playing catch with his friend Asher, he had noticed the apple change in a way he could not describe. On closer investigation, the apple remained the same shape, size, and nondescript shade as always, but then it would briefly change again, though Asher did not seem to notice. Jonas took the apple home to investigate it further, but discovered nothing. The event bewildered him.

In Chapter 4, Jonas meets Asher so that they can do their mandatory volunteer hours together. Children from eight to eleven volunteer at different locations daily to develop skills and get a sense of their occupational interests. Jonas enjoys volunteer hours because they are less regulated than other hours of his day—he gets to choose where he spends them. He volunteers at a variety of places, enjoying the different experiences, and has no idea what his Assignment will be. Today, he goes to the House of the Old, where he notices Asher's bike is parked. In the bathing room, he gives a bath to an elderly woman. He appreciates the sense of safety and trust he gets from the woman—it is against the rules to look at other people naked in any situation, but the rule does not apply to the Old or newchildren. They discuss the release of one of the Old, a man named Roberto. The old woman, Larissa, describes the release as a wonderful celebration—the man's life story was narrated, he was toasted by the other residents of the House of the Old, he made a farewell speech, and then walked blissfully through a special door to be released. Larissa does not know what actually happens when someone is released, but she assumes it is wonderful; she does not understand why children are forbidden to attend.

ANALYSIS

In these chapters, we begin to get a sense of how different Jonas is from other members of his society and also of the degree to which his society discourages differences. Jonas is both physically different, in that his eyes are a very unusual color, and mentally different—he sees the world in a different way, as illustrated by his ability to see the apple change. He is also slightly troubled by some of the strict rules that govern his society. He enjoys the closeness he gets from physical contact with the old woman and does not understand why that kind of closeness is forbidden with other people. He also enjoys having freedom of choice in a way that other people in his community do not seem to appreciate as much. He likes his volunteer hours because he can choose where to spend them, and he takes advantage of that freedom more than most people do. However, although Jonas enjoys freedom, he is still a loyal member of the community. He follows the rules scrupulously, apologizing for stealing the apple as soon as he realizes he has taken it, and he does not-does not think seriously about changing the society's rules.

Lowry uses Jonas's unusual eyes as a metaphor for the unusual way in which he sees the world. His eyes, different from other people's, are a physical representation of his different "vision": he is different on the inside as well as on the outside. The fact that his eyes seem deeper than other people's is also significant. The moment when Jonas sees the apple change will be used later in the novel as an example of Jonas's ability to "see beyond"—to physically see past what other people in his community see, to see qualities of objects that are deeper than the qualities other people see. This ability to see colors when everyone else sees the world in nondescript shades of dark and light is closely related to Jonas's spiritual and emotional ability later in the novel to feel emotions more deeply than other people do.

At this point, the description of how the apple changes is slightly confusing—we have no idea what happens to it when it changes. However, it is the only way that Jonas, with no experience of color, can describe what happens to the apple: it changes, taking on a quality it did not have before. Lowry gives us some hints about what happens to the apple, though. When Jonas describes the apple, he notes that it is the same size and shape as before. He does not use the word "color," to describe its shade. Instead, he uses "nondescript," a word most people would not use to describe the color red. In the novel, the color red comes to be closely aligned to the intense emotions Jonas begins to feel during his training with the Giver. It is a vibrant color, and the community's inability to see it as anything but nondescript is a metaphor for the community's inability to perceive the intensity and beauty of love and other emotions or the excitement of freedom and choice.

These two chapters also reveal the ways in which the society sometimes regards its members as tools rather than as human beings, and the ways in which traditional family relationships are erased. The Birthmothers are treated well only until they have produced their allotted three children for the community. Afterward, they are given a life of hard labor. This custom suggests an extremely practical attitude toward human life: the women are valued for the usefulness of their bodies, and as soon as that usefulness begins to dwindle, their value decreases. The role of mother is not sentimentalized as it is in our society. In fact, very little is sentimentalized: the Old are treated like children and cared for by people with whom they might have had no relationship in their childhood or adulthood. They are kept ignorant—as are most members of the community—about what happens when they are released from the society.

At the same time, young volunteers are able to experience a degree of tenderness with the Old that they cannot experience with anyone else except newchildren. When the Old are no longer functional members of society, they are still treated with kindness and sometimes with respect. Newchildren are treated with tenderness and affection—Jonas's father's concern for Gabriel's welfare is genuine, as is his delight in playing games with the children he nurtures and his sadness at the prospect of releasing them. Although close, lasting relationships with friends and family might not exist, one of the positive qualities of Jonas's community is the entire community's willingness to take care of children, the Old, and each other. Later in the novel, when the negative aspects of Jonas's community come to the fore, it will be helpful to remember that those negative aspects are the price the community pays for a genuinely tranquil and neighborly lifestyle.

CHAPTERS 5–6

SUMMARY

Just as the family practices a telling of feelings at night, they tell their dreams in the morning. Jonas usually does not have a dream to tell, but this morning he has a vivid one: he dreamed that he was in the steamy bathing room at the House of the Old, trying to convince his friend Fiona to take off her clothes and allow him to give her a bath. He remembers feeling a strong "wanting." After sending his sister off to school, Jonas's mother tells him that the feelings he is having are his first Stirrings, something that happens to everyone when they get to be Jonas's age. She gives him a small pill as "treatment" and reminds him to take his pill every morning. Jonas recalls that his parents take the same pill every morning, as do some of his friends. He also recalls hearing announcements made over the loudspeakers reminding children to report their Stirrings for treatment as soon as possible. Jonas is pleased to have grown up enough to have to take the pills, but he tries to remember the dream—he liked the feelings it gave him. However, the pill works quickly, and the pleasures of the dream are gone.

On the first morning of the Ceremony, Jonas and his mother and Lily discuss some of the milestones that children achieve each year— at age seven they get a jacket that they can button themselves, at Eight they begin to volunteer, at nine they get bikes and girls no longer need to wear hair ribbons. At the first Ceremony, the Naming, Jonas's father sits with the other Nurturers, holding the newchildren to be named that year. Gabriel, although he does not weigh enough or sleep through the night well enough to be assigned to a family, has not been released yet—Jonas's father has gotten a year's reprieve for him because their family is taking care of the faltering newchild. In order to do this, each member of the family signed a statement promising not to get attached to Gabriel.

One of the babies named at the Ceremony is a "replacement child" named Caleb. He has been given to a family whose four-year-old son Caleb was "lost" in the river. When he died, the community performed the Ceremony of Loss, chanting his name more and more softly until it seemed to fade away. Now, welcoming the new baby, they chant it louder and louder in the Murmur-of-Replacement Ceremony, which is performed only if a child is lost, not if it is released. The other ceremonies proceed—on the second and final day of the Ceremony, the Nines get their bicycles (everyone cringes when a clumsy child knocks his into the podium, since his clumsiness reflects on his parents' guidance), the Tens' hair is cut. At lunch the Elevens discuss their upcoming Assignments, speculating on what they will do if they get an unsatisfactory Assignment. If a citizen feels that he or she does not fit in with the community, that citizen can apply for Elsewhere and disappear, but Jonas cannot imagine a person feeling that he or she did not fit in, because the community is so well ordered. The Committee of Elders weighs each decision carefully, painstakingly matching adults who applied for spouses to the appropriate spouse and placing newchildren with the appropriate families. Jonas trusts the Committee to give him an appropriate Assignment.

ANALYSIS

Jonas's mother's reaction to his Stirrings and the Murmur-of-Replacement ceremony for the baby Caleb are strong examples of the society's rejection of strong feelings. Jonas's parents recognize the wanting in his dream about Fiona as the first stirrings of the sexual urges that accompany adolescence, and his mother gives him a pill that puts a prompt stop to them. Notice that there is no real shame attached to sexuality in Jonas's society. His dream troubles him because it is unusual, but he is so used to being entirely honest with his family that he tells them all the details of the dream right away, without thinking twice. However, this kind of honesty is only possible because of the limited information each member of the community possesses about life: Jonas has no reason to be ashamed of his sexual feelings because he knows nothing about sex. No one in his society has sexual urges, since they take the pill, so there is no possibility of perverse sexual desires or sexual misconduct. Topics like sexuality, represented by Stirrings, and death, represented by release, are not mystified in Jonas's society as they are in our own Instead, they are dealt with so simply and directly that it does not occur to the citizens to think about them. This probably helps the community to run more smoothly, since the passions that sex and death inspire—lust, jealousy, frustration, and grief—would distract the citizens from their daily work for the community and lead to more selfish relationships or even conflict.

The Murmur-of-Replacement Ceremony is similar to the treatment for the Stirrings. The emotion of grief is subdued in an artificial ceremony in the same way that human sexual urges are subdued by an artificial medication. Instead of allowing Caleb's parents to experience real sadness and pain at the loss of their son, the community encourages them to accept another child named Caleb as a replacement, as if the two children were entirely interchangeable. Note that there is no mention of the word "death"—Caleb has only been "lost." It is possible that the word death is unknown in the community. On close examination, we realize that the Murmur-of-Replacement Ceremony serves the community in the same way that the repression of sexuality does: it de-emphasizes relationships between individuals in the interest of strengthening the individual's ties to the community. If the community thinks of individuals only in terms of their contribution to the community, ignoring the loss of a particular child, citizens will be less likely to form intensely close ties to other individuals. Ties like these could cause citizens to act in their own interests or the interests of their loved ones if those interests ever came into conflict with the interests of the community as a whole. Sexuality can sometimes function this way, too, forging strong, irrational ties between sexual partners.

SUMMARY & ANALYSIS

The Murmur-of-Replacement Ceremony is also noteworthy because of its ritualistic, cultlike qualities. Jonas's community, while it relies highly on logic, precise language, and technology, also relies heavily on ceremony and figurative gestures. The Murmur-of-Replacement Ceremony is based on the metaphor of the community receiving the name of Caleb back into its collective memory, almost as if the citizens were engraving the child's name onto their group consciousness. The experience of many people chanting together with one voice has a powerful psychological effect: it becomes much easier for those people to think of themselves as indistinct from the community. Throughout history, group chanting or singing has been an effective tool to maintain individual loyalty to a group and to prevent dissention. Examples are saying a pledge of allegiance and speaking in a group prayer, and the technique is a hallmark of totalitarian regimes. In analyzing the Murmur-of-Replacement Ceremony, we realize that the members of the community are tied to each other not only by their common goals and interests, but by powerful, pseudo-religious ceremonies and traditions.

Also noteworthy is that Caleb drowned in the river. Early, unplanned deaths of children are exceedingly rare in the community. Few things seem to be beyond anyone's control, but Caleb's death was an accident in a community that does not tolerate accidents (like the Pilot's accidental deviation from his course at the beginning of the novel.) The Murmur-of-Replacement Ceremony helps the community to feel that it has gained some control over the situation, but the accidental drowning remains a powerful event in the book and one that shapes Jonas's ideas about the community's power. The river becomes a symbol of escape from Jonas's society's omniscience and omnipotence, and also a symbol of the strong emotions and desires that the society cannot totally restrain.

CHAPTERS 7–9

SUMMARY

> *"We failed in our last selection,"* the Chief Elder said
> *solemnly.* (See QUOTATIONS, *p. 54*)

Just before the Ceremony of Twelve, Jonas and the other Elevens line up by number—in addition to his or her name, each child has a number that was assigned at birth, showing the order in which he or she was born. Jonas is Nineteen; his friend Fiona is Eighteen. The

Chief Elder, the elected leader of the community, gives a speech before the Ceremony, noting that it is the one time the community recognizes the differences between the children rather than ignoring them as is customary and polite. Jonas watches and listens as his classmates receive their Assignments. His friend Asher is assigned the position of Assistant Director of Recreation after the Chief Elder gives a long and humorous speech about Asher's pleasant, fun-loving nature and the trouble he has had in using precise language. She recalls a time when Asher confused the words "snack" and "smack" at the Childcare Center, and received a smack with the discipline wand every time. She laughs as she remembers that for a while, three-year-old Asher refused to talk at all, but that "he learned . . . [a]nd now his lapses are very few." Jonas is relieved that Asher has received a wonderful Assignment and happy to see that his other classmates are pleased with their Assignments too.

But when Jonas's turn comes, the Chief Elder skips over him, moving from Eighteen to Twenty without acknowledging him. Jonas endures the rest of the Ceremony in horrible embarrassment and worry, wondering what he has done wrong. The audience is concerned too—they are unused to disorder and mistakes. At the end of the Ceremony, the Chief Elder apologizes for causing the audience concern and causing Jonas anguish. She tells him that he has been selected for a very special position, that of Receiver of Memory. The community has only one Receiver at a time, and the current one—a bearded man with pale eyes like Jonas's, sitting with the Committee of Elders—is very old and needs to train a successor. The Chief Elder explains that ten years ago, a new Receiver had been selected, but the selection had been a terrible failure. After Jonas was identified as a possible Receiver, the Elders watched him very carefully and made a unanimous decision to select him, despite the strict selection criteria. To begin with, the candidate for Receiver can be rejected if any of the Elders so much as dreams that he might not be the best selection. The Receiver also needs to possess intelligence, integrity, and courage, as well as the ability to acquire wisdom. Courage is especially important, because as the Receiver, Jonas will experience real pain, something no one else in the community experiences. The job also requires the "Capacity to See Beyond." Jonas does not believe he has this capacity, but then he looks out at the crowd and sees their faces change, the way the apple changed in midair. He realizes he does have it after all. The Chief Elder thanks him for his childhood, and the crowd accepts him as the new Receiver by chanting his name louder and louder. Jonas feels gratitude, pride, and fear at the same time.

Although his training, which will keep him apart from other members of the community, has not yet begun, Jonas immediately begins to feel isolated from his friends and family, who treat him differently from before, though very respectfully. At home, his family is quieter than usual, though his parents tell him that they are very honored that he has been selected as Receiver. When he asks about the previous, failed selection, they reluctantly tell him that the name of the female selected ten years ago is Not-to-Be-Spoken, indicating the highest degree of disgrace.

Before bed, Jonas looks over the single sheet of paper in his Assignment folder. He learns that he is exempted from rules governing rudeness—he can ask anyone any question he likes and expect an answer—that he is not allowed to discuss his training with anyone, that he is not allowed to tell his dreams to anyone, that he cannot apply for medication unless it is for an illness unrelated to his training, that he cannot apply for release, and that he is allowed to lie. He also learns that he will have very little time for recreation and wonders what will happen to his friendships. The other instructions disturb him too—he cannot imagine being rude, nor can he imagine not having access to medication. In his community, medicine is always instantly delivered to stop pain of any kind, and the idea that his training involves excruciating pain is almost incomprehensible. He cannot imagine lying, either, having been trained since childhood to speak with total precision and accuracy, even avoiding exaggeration and figures of speech. He wonders if anyone else in his community is allowed to lie too.

Analysis

The Chief Elder's description of Asher's childhood troubles gives us our first concrete example of the real cruelty that keeps the community so peaceful and happy. Though Asher seems to be a well-adjusted child, the idea that a normal three-year-old child's confusion of two similar words could be so systematically and coldheartedly punished is difficult to accept. When a child whose language development had been progressing normally suddenly regresses into silence from constant physical punishment, that is evidence of severe trauma. Several events in the novel have already made us wonder if the peace and order of the society is worth the sacrifices its members have to make—sacrifices of individual freedom, deep personal relationships, and sexual pleasure—but Asher's punishments demonstrate the severity of those sacrifices and help us to understand how intolerant the community is of differences and personality quirks.

Of course, the Ceremony of Twelve is the time when the community celebrates differences, and for Jonas it is the time when his own differences are made uncomfortably clear. His anguish and discomfort at being singled out at the Ceremony is only his first taste of the isolation he will experience as the new Receiver—the only member of the community whose life experience is appreciably different from anyone else's. His family's quiet respect for him and his friends' distant behavior contribute to this growing feeling of isolation. Jonas is already different—already he has the ability to see beyond—but until now, he has not felt particularly different, and it has not occurred to him to criticize or question many of the community's rules and practices. Interestingly, the role he is assigned, in accentuating his differences, encourages him to question those rules and practices, as he begins to do at the end of Chapter 9. The rules that permit him to act differently—he is permitted to be rude and to lie, among other things—encourage him to think differently: his permission to lie makes him wonder for the first time if other people in his society are permitted to lie too. Jonas loses some of his faith and trust in the members of his community. This slight loss of trust reminds us how dangerous it is to the structure of Jonas's society to permit free choice or to encourage free thought.

The old Receiver's eyes are the same color as Jonas's and the newchild Gabriel's. Since Jonas's eyes already have a metaphorical meaning in the story, symbolizing his uniqueness, his isolation from his community, and his depth of vision (both physical and mental), we immediately associate those qualities with the Receiver too. The shared eye color links the Receiver and Jonas, suggesting that Jonas was destined to be the Receiver even before his abilities were recognized by the Committee of Elders. This destiny could be genetic—the genes giving Jonas and the Receiver light eyes might also govern their personality traits and their abilities to see beyond—or it could be more mystical in nature, with the light eyes serving as a mark of special, mysterious powers. Lowry's use of light eyes as a kind of talisman indicating powers that Jonas cannot explain or understand foreshadows Jonas's training later in the novel, when the memories of the Receiver, as well as the way he transmits them, take on a mystical, inexplicable quality that demonstrates how little the other members of the community understand them.

The fact that the newchild Gabriel has the same color eyes as Jonas and the Receiver indicates that his character will play a very significant role in the novel. His eyes have already marked him as unusual, and they have already linked him to Jonas, but the fact that he shares qualities with the Receiver suggests that he is even more special—that he, too, might be gifted with mysterious powers.

CHAPTERS 10–11

SUMMARY

Jonas reports to the Annex of the House of the Old for his first day of training. An Attendant admits him to the Receiver's living area, which is locked to ensure the Receiver's privacy, even though no one else in the community locks their doors. The living area is more luxurious than average, and its walls are lined with hundreds of thick, beautifully bound books, very different from the three reference volumes (dictionary, community volume, Book of Rules) available in every other household. Jonas cannot imagine what could be inside them. He meets the Receiver, who greets him as the new Receiver of Memory and tells him that although he, the old Receiver, is not as old as he looks, he will need to use the last of his strength to train Jonas. He says that the process involves transmitting all of the memories he has of the past to Jonas. Jonas wonders why listening to stories from the old man's childhood is so important that he cannot just do it in his spare time, leaving him free to work at an adult job in the community. The Receiver replies that the memories he will give Jonas are not just memories from his childhood. They are the memories of the entire world, going back through generations and generations of Receivers. These memories of communities and worlds before Jonas's community bring wisdom and help the community to shape its future. The Receiver feels weighed down by so many memories and compares the feeling to a sled slowing down as it has to push against more and more accumulated snow.

Jonas does not understand the comparison, because he has never seen snow or a sled. The Receiver decides to transmit the memory of snow to him. He instructs Jonas to take off his tunic and lie face-down on the bed. Then he goes to the speaker, which is just like the speaker that transmits announcements in every house, and turns it off, something that no one else in the community can do. He places his hands on Jonas's back, and Jonas begins to feel the sensation of cold air, then of snowflakes touching his face. He experiences the wonderful sensation of going downhill on a sled, feeling the exhilaration of movement and speed even though he has never felt snow or strong wind or even a hill. In his community, all hills have been leveled to make transportation easier, and snow disappeared with the onset of climate control that made agriculture more efficient. When the experience is over, the Receiver tells Jonas that the memory is a very distant one, from before the time when "we went to Sameness." Jonas says that he wishes snow and hills still existed, and asks the Receiver why he does not use his great power to bring them back. The Receiver answers that great honor is not the same thing as great power. He then gives Jonas the memory of sunshine, and Jonas perceives the word for "sunshine" at the same time that he perceives the sensation of it. Afterward he asks about the pain he will experience, and the Receiver gives him the mild pain of a sunburn in order to get him used to the idea. Jonas finds the experience interesting, if not pleasant. When he leaves, he asks the Receiver what he should call him now that he, Jonas, is the new Receiver. The Receiver, drained from their day's work, says to call him the Giver.

ANALYSIS

The comparative luxury of the Giver's living area reflects his honored position in the community, but it also sets him apart: he needs different surroundings in order to do his job. He spends most of his life in the world of the past, so he probably craves the sensual and aesthetic comforts that the pre-Sameness world valued. His job also involves enduring pain, so as compensation his environment is comfortable and luxurious. One of the luxuries seems to be his enormous collection of books. Jonas cannot imagine what the books contain: he only knows the three reference books his family owns. We realize that Jonas has never read a book for pleasure, and this makes sense: reading is a solitary, isolating pursuit. Sitting alone with a book all day encourages people to draw too deeply into themselves rather than participate in activities that help the community or strengthen social bonds between community members.

The luxury of the Giver's apartment and his extensive library remind us of similar living quarters in other dystopian novels, such as 1984 and *Brave New World*. In these novels, most of the population lives according to the dystopian community's rules, foregoing individual pursuits for the community's gain, submitting to government surveillance, and substituting group mentality for intellectual inquiry. But in each novel, characters who are part of the elite classes ignore the rules that they themselves helped to create, preferring the artifacts of a culture they destroyed or rejected to the amusements of the society they govern and maintain. This suggests that great works of art, often inspired by passion, pain, and other disorderly influences, are always powerful and relevant, even in societies that claim to have gotten rid of passion and pain.

Although the Giver is not as hypocritical as the elite characters in 1984 and *Brave New World*—they read Shakespeare and Plato for their own pleasure, while he uses his knowledge to help the community make decisions—the Giver's library and the Giver himself represent this same idea in Lowry's novel. Although the society has rejected the powerful emotions and dangerous freedom of thought that produced great works of art in the past, it cannot function without the wisdom contained in those works or without the Giver's wisdom. The fact that books, memory, love, and pain must exist somewhere in the society, even if they exist only in one room or in the mind of one man, shows that these things are more valuable and timeless than Jonas's community would like to think. Humans cannot escape them.

When the Giver explains that snow, hills, and sleds all vanished when the community went to Sameness, he gives a name to Jonas's society for the first time. We have already noticed that everyone in the community strives to be the same, but applying the term Sameness to the physical details of the environment as well as to the behavior and psychology of the inhabitants helps to explain the rationale behind the community philosophy. The hills have been leveled and the climate controlled because it makes farming and transportation more efficient and life much easier. Long ago, the same people who made these decisions must have thought that life would be more efficient if everyone looked and thought and dressed the same too: it was a practical decision. At the same time, the physical Sameness of the environment serves as a powerful metaphor for the emotional and intellectual monotony of life in the community. There are no extremes of cold or heat, no exhilarating sled rides or depressing moments. The land is as flat and changeless as the inhabitants' lives.

The Giver's method of transmitting memories is also significant in this section. He can give Jonas the experience of a ride on a sled simply by placing his hands on his back, a technique that seems magical, or at least extremely ritualistic. All of the events connected with memory in *The Giver* seem to be suffused with religion and ritual: the ritualistic Murmur-of-Replacement Ceremony, Jonas's acceptance by the community as the new Receiver, the Giver's mysterious laying on of hands that produces powerful visions. In some ways, the Giver is the closest thing to a priest in the community, able to touch the mind and soul with the touch of his hands, just as he and Jonas can "see" deeper aspects of human experience with their unusual eyes.

Note that the Giver touches Jonas's bare back with his bare hands, a highly unusual action in a society that forbids citizens to see each other's nakedness. We are reminded of Jonas's contact with the old woman, Larissa, when he bathed her in the tub. He felt a strong sense of trust and connection that was rare in his daily interactions with friends and family. Now that sense of trust and human connection is closely tied with the receiving of memories, suggesting that memory creates and maintains close, meaningful human relationships and that those relationships do not exist in a world without memory.

CHAPTERS 12–13

SUMMARY

We really have to protect people from wrong choices.
(*See* QUOTATIONS, *p. 55*)

After Jonas receives his first memory, he finds that it is not too hard to obey the rules that come with his position. His family is used to his not dreaming frequently, so they do not question him much at dream-telling time. His friends are so busy describing their own training experiences that he can just sit still and listen, knowing that he could not even begin to explain what happens in his training. As they bicycle to the House of the Old together, he talks with his friend Fiona about her training as a Caretaker of the Old and notices her hair change the way the apple changed. At the Giver's living space, Jonas tells him about the changes, wondering if that is what the Giver means by seeing beyond. The Giver says that for him, his first experiences with seeing beyond took a different form, one that Jonas would not understand yet. He asks Jonas to remember the sled from yesterday, and Jonas notices that the sled has the same strange quality as Fiona's hair and the apple—it does not change as they did, it just has the quality. The Giver tells Jonas that he is beginning to see the color red, explaining that at one time everything in the world had color as well as shape and size. The reason that the sled is just red, instead of turning red, is that it is a memory from a time when color existed. Jonas remarks that red is beautiful and wonders why his community got rid of it, and the Giver tells him that in order to gain control of certain things, the society had to let go of others. Jonas says that they should not have done so, and the Giver tells Jonas that he is quickly acquiring wisdom.

As Jonas's training progresses, he learns about all the different colors and begins to see them fleetingly in his daily life. He decides that it is unfair that nothing in his society has color—he wants to have the freedom to choose between things that are different. Then he realizes that if people had the power to make choices, they might make the wrong choices. It would be unsafe to allow people to choose their spouse or their job, but he still feels frustrated. He wishes his friends and family could see the world the way he sees it. He makes Asher stare at a flowerbed, hoping Asher will notice the colors, but Asher becomes uncomfortable. Another time, after the Giver transmits a memory of an elephant mourning the death of another elephant that was brutally killed by poachers, he tries to give the memory to Lily, hoping that she will understand that her toy elephant is a representation of something that was once real and majestic and awe-inspiring. It does not work.

Jonas's training makes him curious. He asks if the Giver is allowed to have a spouse, and the Giver says that he did have a spouse once—now she lives with the Childless Adults, as almost all adults do when their children are grown and their family units have dissolved. The Giver tells him that being the Receiver makes family life difficult—Jonas will not be able to share his memories or books with his spouse or children. The Giver tells Jonas that his whole life will be nothing more than the memories he possesses. He occasionally will appear before the Committee of Elders to give them advice, but his primary function is to contain all the painful memories that the community cannot endure. When the new Receiver who was selected ten years before failed, all the memories she had received returned to the community, and the whole community suffered until the memories were assimilated. The Giver tells Jonas that his instructors know nothing, despite their scientific knowledge, because all of their knowledge is meaningless without the memories the Giver carries. Jonas notices that the Giver's memories give him pain, and he wonders what causes it. He also wonders what lies Elsewhere, beyond his community. The Giver decides to give Jonas a memory of strong pain so that he can bear some of the Giver's pain for him.

ANALYSIS

Jonas's alienation from his community intensifies as he begins to question the values with which he grew up. As his physical vision deepens and changes, allowing him to see the color red, his metaphorical vision also deepens and changes, allowing him to see how empty the lives of his friends and family are compared to his own. He tries to transmit the idea of color to Asher and the memory of elephants to Lily, but he fails: unlike Jonas, his friends are physically incapable of seeing color, and they have no reason to believe that elephants exist. Perhaps Jonas could give Asher and Lily these sensations if he could manage to touch their skin, but the rules and conventions of his society make that impossible. Physical nakedness becomes a metaphor for emotional bareness: Jonas's friends cannot share his experience because their society makes them reluctant to show their bare skin, but it is equally impossible for them to show their bare emotions because they do not even know they have them. In order to share Jonas's experience, Asher and Lily would need to trust him totally. They would need to be entirely open to the ideas he shared with them, and the society they have grown up in has made that kind of openness almost impossible. Jonas's experiences with them foreshadow the Giver's explanation, later in this section, that the Receiver cannot share his experiences and knowledge with his loved ones. It is forbidden, but it is also almost physically impossible.

These chapters draw close connections between color and emotion—another example of Lowry's use of physical imagery to symbolize deeper, nonphysical sensations. The memories that the Giver has transmitted to Jonas so far are mostly memories of the natural world or of solitary experiences, and yet Jonas is gaining a stronger sense of the complex emotions. When he tries to transmit the color red to Asher and the idea of an elephant to Lily, he is really trying to transmit the intense feelings of pleasure and surprise that the world of color has opened up to him or the sense of pity, awe, and love that he got from the relationship between the two elephants. When Jonas apologizes for hurting Lily with his efforts to make her understand what a real elephant is like, she answers with indifference: "'ccept your apology." The contrast between her casual treatment of an apology—a social formula that was once an expression of real pain and regret—and Jonas's emotional response to the elephants is strong, and illustrates that the members of Jonas's community are immune to powerful feelings. Although the community insists on precision of language, many words in the society have lost the emotional resonance that was once so important to their meaning.

When Jonas and the Giver discuss the reason that there are no colors in the community anymore, Jonas agrees with the Giver's statement that "[w]e gained control of many things. But we had to let go of others." He is angry at first that the lack of color makes it difficult to exercise free choice, but when he realizes that being able to choose between a red jersey and a blue jersey might lead people to want to choose spouses and jobs, he concedes that people have to be protected from "wrong choices." This principle explains the community's extreme emphasis on Sameness: although choosing one color over another based on personal preference might seem innocent enough, it would be dangerous to the structure of Jonas's community to allow people even the minor pleasure of making an aesthetic choice. In order to keep them from yearning for more and more personal freedom, the society must make the sensation of choice totally alien to the community members. This strict limitation of all choice indicates that the current state of the society is unnatural: drastic measures must be taken to maintain its artificial order, peace, and lack of personal liberty.

The Giver's attitude toward science, combined with the mysterious way in which the failed Receiver's memories returned to plague the community, confirms the dichotomy we noticed earlier between the mystical, religious nature of memory and the logical order of the community and of Sameness. It is possible that Lowry chose to associate memory with magic and mystery in order to give her readers a stronger sense of how strange and inexplicable memory is for the members of the community. Since they have no experience with emotion, pain, history, or love, these ideas must seem as strange and improbable to them as magical powers seem to us. In our own world, where we acknowledge the existence of emotions, we still have trouble explaining human desires and behavior with science. In Jonas's world, the significance of these forces are almost totally ignored, and somebody who understands them and can communicate them is someone who truly defies logic, science, and everything in the known world.

CHAPTERS 14–16

SUMMARY

The Giver transmits the memory of another ride on a sled, only this time the sled loses control and Jonas experiences pain and nausea from a badly broken leg. The pain lingers after the experience is over, but the Giver is not allowed to give him relief-of-pain, and Jonas limps home and goes to bed early. Forbidden to share his feelings with his family, he feels isolated, realizing that they have never known intense pain. Over the next days, the Giver transmits more and more painful memories, always ending the day with a memory of pleasure. After experiencing starvation, Jonas asks why these horrible memories need to be preserved, and the Giver explains that they bring wisdom: once, for example, the community wanted to increase the number of children allowed to each family, but the Giver remembered the hunger that overpopulation brings and advised against it. Jonas wonders why the whole community cannot share the pain of these important memories, and the Giver tells him that this is the reason the position of Receiver is so honored—the community does not want to be burdened and pained by memories. Jonas wants to change things, but the Giver reminds him that the situation has been the same for generations, and that there is very little hope for change.

Meanwhile, the newchild Gabriel is developing well, but still cannot sleep through the night. Jonas's father worries that he will have to be released after all. He mentions that the Nurturing Center will probably have to make another release first, though: a Birthmother is expecting twin males, and if they are identical, one will have to be released. Jonas wonders what happens to children who are released. Is someone waiting for them Elsewhere to bring them up and take care of them? He asks his parents to let Gabriel sleep in his room that night so that he can share the responsibility of caring for him. When Gabriel wakes up crying, Jonas pats his back while remembering a wonderful sail on a lake transmitted to him by the Giver. He realizes that he is unwittingly transmitting the memory to Gabriel and stops himself. Later, he transmits the whole memory and Gabriel stops crying and sleeps. Jonas wonders if he has done the right thing.

The next day, Jonas finds the Giver in incredible pain, and the Giver asks him to take some of the pain away. The Giver transmits the terrible memory of a battlefield covered with groaning, dying men and horses. Jonas, himself horribly wounded, gives water to a young soldier and then watches him die. After this memory, Jonas never wants to go back to the Annex for more wisdom and pain, but he does, and the Giver transmits beautiful memories—birthday parties, art museums, horseback riding, camping—that celebrate individuality, brilliant colors, the bond between people and animals, and solitude, all things absent from Jonas's society. He asks the Giver what his favorite memory is, and the Giver transmits a memory of a family—grandparents, parents, young children—opening presents at Christmas. Jonas has never heard of grandparents. In his community, parents cease to be a part of children's lives once the children have grown up—children do not even know when their parents are released. He understands that his organized society works well, but he felt a feeling in the room that he liked. The Giver tells him that the feeling is love, and Jonas says that he wishes his own family could be like the family in the memory and that the Giver could be his grandparent. At home that evening, he asks his parents if they love him. They laugh and tell him to use more precise language: the word "love" is so general that it is almost meaningless. They enjoy him, and they are proud of him, but they cannot say they love him. Jonas pretends to agree with them, but secretly he does not understand. That night, he tells little Gabriel—who can only sleep through the night when Jonas gives him memories—that if things were different in the community, there could be colors and grandparents and love. The next morning, Jonas decides to stop taking his morning pill.

ANALYSIS

The Giver's role in making decisions for the community explains the importance of his position. He is not just a mystic who holds onto out-of-date emotions and sensations despite that they are no longer useful to the community. He is the only person in the community who can prevent mistakes from being repeated, which is the practical function of history. In this sense, the Giver's job is as practical and necessary as any other in the community: through his wisdom, he keeps the community well fed and well ordered just as much as the Fish Hatchery Attendant or the Nurturer do.

But the Giver's presence somehow still undermines the impression of logic and order that we get from the community. The Committee of Elders does not base its decisions on real logic or reason because it lacks the resources to make any kind of considered decision about anything (the characters in the novel constantly make jokes about the Committee's painfully slow decision-making process.) The resource they need is experience, and as a culture, Jonas's community lacks experience: it destroys experience. On the issue of adding a third child to every family, the Committee did not take the Giver's advice because they thought about his argument and realized that too many people *would* lead to a lack of resources. They took his advice on blind faith, because they lacked any other way of making a choice. Choice is impossible without memory, just as freedom is impossible without choice.

The pain Jonas experiences isolates him further from his family and friends when he realizes that they have never experienced any real pain, but at the same time it drives him to try to forge deeper connections with other people—his parents and the newchild Gabriel. Jonas learns about love when he receives the memory of the family at Christmas, but he learns about true compassion in his experience on the battlefield. The contrast between his painful memories and his pleasurable memories is strong, but not as strong as the contrast between the memories and the colorless realities of life in Jonas's community. Jonas's pain gives new depth and value to his pleasure. We realize that the citizens of the community lack the capacity for pleasure not only because it would destabilize the society, but also because it is impossible to experience deep pleasure without having experienced pain, and they have consciously eliminated pain.

Jonas's attempt to reach out to his parents fails when they tell him that they do not love him. They emphasize precision of language, but that particular kind of precision actually limits the expressiveness of their language. Jonas knows that the feeling of love exists and that to reduce it to simpler feelings, like enjoyment and pride, is useless as well as imprecise. We see how the "precise" language the community uses for things often drains them of meaning: "pride" and "enjoyment" do not express the feeling of love, and "release" does not express the idea of death. Although we do not know for sure at this point in the novel that release is death, we have a strong suspicion. The use of the word "release," though it might be technically correct, makes it too easy to ignore what really happens when someone dies.

Jonas's attempts to connect with Gabriel are much more successful. In possibly breaking the rules of his Assignment by transmitting memories to the baby, Jonas is also breaking a more unspoken rule against forming too close a bond with an individual. After experiencing the Christmas scene, with grandparents who remain part of their children's lives long after their practical function as parents is finished, Jonas craves the kind of close, selfish relationship with another human that his society discourages. He says he understands that this kind of close family life is a "dangerous" way to live, trying to justify his statement by saying that the candles and fire in the loving family's living room are dangerous to have indoors. The fire and candles, however, serve as symbols for the warmth and light of human love, and that love is dangerous because it would upset the delicate balance of Jonas's society. But warmth and light are necessary for survival, and Jonas begins to feel that love is too. It is important to note that the depiction of the family at Christmas seems to idealize the traditional family group and reject the system of Nurturers and Caretakers presented by Jonas's community. This rejection is based on the lack of love and lasting relationships to be found within Jonas's community, and not necessarily on its nontraditional structure. This need for close relationships and desire for the strong emotion that accompanies them influences Jonas's decision to stop taking his pills.

Jonas stops taking the pills just so he can experience the sensation of wanting something, not because he has hopes to start a sexual relationship with another person. He wants to feel capable of making choices, and he wants to want things—nothing will change if he does not want it to very badly. The only person he can connect with, besides the Giver, is the newchild Gabriel. As a new human being, Gabriel symbolizes the hope for change. Jonas can give Gabriel his memories and his love because he has not yet been conditioned to live like everyone else in the community.

CHAPTERS 17–18

SUMMARY

Four weeks after Jonas stops taking his pills, an unscheduled holiday is declared in the community. His Stirrings have returned, and he has pleasurable dreams that make him feel a little guilty, but he refuses to give up the heightened feelings that the Stirrings and his wonderful memories have given him. Jonas realizes that he now experiences a new depth of feeling. He understands that the feelings his family and friends call anger and sadness and happiness are nothing like the feelings of rage and despair and joy he knows through his memories. On this particular holiday, Jonas refuses to participate with his friends in a game of good guys and bad guys, because he recognizes it as a war game. He tries to explain to his friends that the game is a cruel mockery of a horrible reality, but they are only puzzled and annoyed. He leaves his friends, knowing that they cannot understand his feelings or even return the strong love that he feels for them. At home, he feels better when he sees Gabe, who has learned to walk and to say his own name. His father talks about the upcoming release of one of the identical twins that will be born the next day. Jonas asks his father if he will actually take the newchild Elsewhere, and his father says no. He will only select the child with the lowest birthweight, perform a Ceremony of Release, and wave goodbye. Someone else will come and get him from Elsewhere. Lily speculates about two identical twins growing up with the same name, one here and one Elsewhere.

The next day, Jonas asks the Giver if he thinks about release. The Giver says he thinks of his own when he is in great pain, but that he cannot apply for release until Jonas is trained. Jonas cannot ask for release either, a rule that was created after the failure of the new Receiver ten years ago. At Jonas's insistence, the Giver tells him what happened. The failed Receiver was intelligent and eager to learn, and her name was Rosemary. The Giver tells Jonas that he loved her, and that he loves Jonas in the same way. When Rosemary's training began, she loved experiencing new things, and the Giver started with happy memories that would make her laugh. But she wanted more difficult memories. The Giver could not bring himself to give her physical pain, but at her insistence he gave her loneliness, loss, poverty, and fear. After a very hard session, she kissed the Giver's cheek and left. He never saw her again. Later, he learned that she had applied for release that day. Jonas knows that he cannot apply for release, but he asks the Giver what would happen if he accidentally drowned in the river, carrying a year's worth of memories with him. The Giver tells him it would be a disaster: his memories would not be lost, but instead all of the people in the community would have them, and they would not be able to deal with them. The Giver becomes thoughtful and says that if that happened, perhaps he could help the community to deal with the memories in the same way that he helps Jonas, but that he would need more time to think about it. He warns Jonas to stay away from the river, just in case.

ANALYSIS

The attitudes that Asher and Lily have toward violence and release are typical, since neither understands what violence and death really entail. For Lily in particular, and also for Jonas, the precision of the word "release" allows her to totally ignore the pain, suffering, and sadness that often accompany death, since she literally believes that released children are raised by families in other communities. Treating release as only slightly more serious than a journey is made possible by the word itself, since it can have other meanings besides death.

Jonas, too, still does not understand what release really means. Since Jonas suffered death and pain through the Giver's memories, we might expect him to suspect the truth. However, though Jonas is well versed in the ways of the world before Sameness, his memories have taught him nothing about life in his community. His time with the Giver has made him aware of what his community does not offer (color, desire, pain), but it has not revealed any of the secrets concealed beneath his society's veneer of tranquility. Jonas does not associate the idea of release with his new understanding of physical pain. Instead, he is curious because his recent exposure to psychological pain—to real loneliness and real happiness—makes him wonder about the difficult separation from the community, and his new isolation that makes him wonder about the ultimate isolation of release.

Rosemary, the name of the failed Receiver, is also the name of an herb that is associated with remembrance. Rosemary was an appropriate choice for Receiver, but the fact that after her failure it was forbidden to speak her name again is telling: after their unpleasant experience dealing with all of Rosemary's released memories, the community wanted nothing to do with remembrance, and their rejection of her name constitutes a double rejection of memory.

It is interesting to note that though the Giver could not bear to give Rosemary physical pain, he allowed himself to give her pain that some people might consider to be far worse than physical pain. He subjects Jonas to a broken leg, starvation, and war wounds, but these agonies eventually subside. Apparently—at least at the time—he thought Rosemary was better suited to endure loneliness and fear. The community seems to have eliminated gender roles when it went to Sameness, and yet a few traditional gender stereotypes remain: girls and boys have different hairstyles, for example, and the Giver at least seems to think girls should be treated with more physical gentleness.

When Jonas discusses the fact that he is forbidden to request release with the Giver, it is interesting to think of the complex meanings that the word "release" has in this book. Release means death, and therefore it connotes sadness and loss to us, but to the community someone's release can be cause for joy, sadness, or enormous shame. For Jonas, who has been exposed to feelings and memories that no one else in the community besides the Giver shares, the word is even more complicated. Release from the community could be shameful or painful, but it would also mean a kind of escape from an oppressive, limiting society.

Although he is the first Receiver to be denied the right to request release, Jonas also becomes the first one to crave and to accomplish real release: an escape from the society. The release that Rosemary sought is possible for Jonas, without using any euphemisms. As we will see in later chapters, Jonas manages to physically leave the community alive, to actually explore Elsewhere. Far from being the only member of the community who cannot be released, he is the only one who can and will be released. At the same time, Jonas has already been released from the hold that the community keeps on all of its citizens, and his Assignment as the Receiver is the very thing that released him. He can see beyond the rules and conventions of the society he lives in, and he can feel things that no one else in the society can feel.

When Jonas alludes to the child Caleb's death in the river, he is imagining situations that are beyond the community's control: accidents that the community cannot prevent or even expect. Though Jonas is not consciously thinking of ways to subvert the society, the mention of the river reminds us and the Giver that the community is fragile in many ways and still vulnerable to natural disasters and accidents. The Giver warns Jonas not to go near the river, but even as he says this, Jonas is beginning to consider the river a way out. Since it flows through the community from Elsewhere, the river is a physical symbol of escape from the community, and the untamed natural power that it possesses represents the way a tide of unexpected feelings and sensations could change the community for good.

CHAPTERS 19–20

SUMMARY

> *"There's nothing we can do. It's always been this way."*
> *(See QUOTATIONS, p. 56)*

Jonas explains that he is curious about release because his father released a newchild that day. The Giver says that he wishes that newchildren were not released, and Jonas reminds him that it would be confusing to have two identical people walking around. The Giver tells Jonas that, as Receiver, he is allowed to have access to any information he wants and that if he wants to watch a release, he can. Since all private ceremonies are recorded, Jonas can even watch his father's release of the newchild that morning. Jonas agrees to watch it, and the Giver calls the recording up on a video screen. Jonas watches as his father weighs the twins, then gently injects something into a vein in the smaller one's head. The newchild twitches and lies still, and Jonas realizes that it is dead. He recognizes the gestures and posture of the boy that he saw die on the battlefield. Horrified, he watches his father place the body in a garbage chute and wave goodbye. The Giver tells Jonas that he watched the recording of Rosemary's release. She had been told to roll up her sleeve, but she chose to inject herself.

Jonas is overcome by pain and horror when he realizes what release really is. He starts crying and refuses to go home to his family, knowing that his father lied to him about what would happen to the newchild. He cannot believe that his friend Fiona efficiently kills the Old when they are released. The Giver allows Jonas to spend the night with him and tries to explain that the people of his community do not feel things the way that he and Jonas do. He tells Jonas that Jonas has helped him to decide that things have to change, that the memories have to be shared.

The Giver and Jonas come up with a plan: Jonas will escape from the community, leaving all his memories for the people of the community. Jonas begs the Giver to come with him, but the Giver explains that someone needs to stay to help the others deal with those memories, or the community will be thrown into utter chaos. Jonas says that he does not want to care about the other people, but he knows that the only reason he and the Giver devised the plan is because they do care about the others. The Giver tells Jonas that he himself is too weak to make the journey anyway. He cannot even see colors anymore. Jonas asks the Giver about his early experiences with seeing beyond, how they were different from Jonas's own, and the Giver tells him that he heard beyond. He heard music, something Jonas would not understand because the Giver has kept music to himself.

For the next two weeks, the Giver plans to transmit memories of courage and strength to help Jonas with his journey. At midnight on the night before the Ceremony, Jonas will slip out of his house with an extra set of clothing, which he will hide by the riverbank next to his bicycle. The next day, the Giver will order a vehicle for a visit to another community, hide Jonas in the storage area, and give him a head start on his journey to Elsewhere. The Giver will tell the community that Jonas has been lost in the river, they will perform the Ceremony of Loss, and he will help them bear Jonas's memories. The Giver tells Jonas that afterward, he will be with his daughter, Rosemary.

ANALYSIS

When Jonas finally understands that his father killed the newchild when he released it, we understand why he is horrified, feeling that his father has betrayed his trust. As readers, we feel along with Jonas that his community is cruel to condone the murder of children and the Old. However, the death of the infant seems infinitely more horrific to Jonas than it would to almost anyone else who lived in his community: Jonas and the Giver are the only people who know what death really means. Jonas is horrified because the movements of the dying baby echo the movements of the dying boy in the memory, and he associates those movements with pain, thirst, and misery. If Lily or Asher or even Fiona were to see the death throes of the baby, they might not understand what the baby is feeling—and in fact the baby probably does not feel much when it dies, since Jonas's father is so gentle. But a year's worth of transmitted memories have taught Jonas to think of death as we think of death—something horrible to be avoided at all costs.

Jonas's unequivocal disgust at the baby's death must be heightened by the fact that there is no good reason to eliminate the baby, except that it looks too much like its brother: the baby's life would not have been extremely difficult, nor would it have put his brother's life in danger. It just would have made life a little bit more inconvenient for the members of the community. Jonas does not recoil at the baby's death just because he senses that it is in pain. He has also grown to understand the worth of an individual human being as well as how humans in the past struggled to preserve life in the face of war, sickness, and natural disasters. It disgusts him to see his father throwing away the precious uniqueness that the baby probably has to offer, and the casual nature of his death seems like an insult to all of the people who have struggled so hard to survive.

At this point in the novel, Jonas's emotional reaction to the baby's death overcomes him, to the point where he ceases to care what happens to the other members of the society. Having grown up acting only for the community's good, with little thought to any desires that might not serve the community, Jonas now holds the opposite point of view. He only wants to rescue himself and the Giver from the dangerous, suffocating atmosphere of the community. Instead of having no strong emotions at all, he has given himself entirely to his emotions. Now the Giver has to restrain him, using logic to explain that the Giver has to stay to help the community if the plan is to have any effect. When he explains this to Jonas, the Giver demonstrates an ideal blend of logical, orderly thought and human compassion. Jonas and the Giver are acting in the best interests of the community, but they are using their emotions and compassion—things that the community rejects—to help it.

CHAPTERS 21–23

SUMMARY

> He heard people singing. Behind him, across vast
> distances of space and time, from the place he had left,
> he thought he heard music too. But perhaps it was
> only an echo.
>
> (See QUOTATIONS, p. 57)

Instead of waiting two weeks as he and the Giver had planned, Jonas is forced to escape right away. At the evening meal, his father tells the family that he tried to see if Gabriel could sleep through the night at the Nurturing Center, and that the newchild had cried all night. The staff, including Jonas's father, voted to release him the next day. Jonas cannot allow this to happen, so he takes some leftover food and his father's bicycle, which has a child seat, and leaves, relying on his own courage and strength instead of on the memories that the Giver had promised. Jonas has broken serious rules against leaving his dwelling at night and taking food. After riding all night, he and

Gabe rest during the day, hiding from the planes that fly overhead searching for them. He transmits memories of exhaustion to Gabriel in order to make him sleep during the day, and in order to avoid the heat-seeking technology of the planes, he transmits memory of intense cold to both of them so that their body heat does not show up on the planes' devices. After several days, when Jonas and Gabriel have left all communities far behind, the planes come less frequently.

The landscape around them begins to change: the terrain becomes bumpy and irregular, and Jonas falls and twists his ankle. He sees waterfalls and wildlife, all new things to him after a life of Sameness. He is happy to see beautiful things, but worries that he and Gabe might starve, since there is no sign of cultivated land anywhere around. He catches some fish in a makeshift net and gathers some berries, but they are only just enough. If he had stayed in the community, he would have had enough to eat, and he realizes that in choosing to leave, he chose to starve. But in the community he would have been hungry for feelings and color, and Gabriel would have died. The weather changes, and Jonas feels cold and hunger and pain from his twisted ankle. But he suspects that Elsewhere is not far away and hopes that he will be able to keep Gabriel alive.

One day, it begins to snow, and Jonas's bicycle cannot climb the steep hill that rises before them. Jonas has lost most of the memories he received from the Giver, but he tries to remember sunshine and the feeling of warmth that it gives. When it comes, he transmits the feeling to Gabriel, and it helps them make it up the hill on foot, despite the intense cold and hunger they feel. When he can no longer remember sunshine, and is almost totally numb with cold, Jonas remembers his friends and family and the Giver, and the happiness their memories give him helps him to reach the top. He recognizes the snow-covered summit of the hill, and somehow finds a sled waiting for him there. He gets in the sled and steers himself and Gabe to the bottom, toward warm, twinkling lights that glow from the windows of houses. He feels certain that the families in those houses, where they kept memories and celebrated love, were waiting for him and Gabe. Ahead of him, he hears singing for the first time in his life, and he thinks that he hears the music behind him too.

ANALYSIS

In the last chapters of *The Giver*, Jonas truly begins to exist in the world of his memories. This begins when he makes the drastic choice to escape ahead of schedule with Gabriel in tow. Jonas is aware that he is breaking rules against leaving his dwelling and taking food, but in reality he is breaking a much more serious rule, one on which his entire society is based. He is making choices for himself as an individual, and in doing this he is making himself important as an individual rather than as a member of a society. He is also making the choice that Gabriel's individual life is more precious than the convenience of the community. At the same time, however, Jonas is making choices that affect the entire community, acting in what he considers their self-interest. This choice, though, opposes another fundamental rule of the society: everything should be done to avoid pain and discomfort. Jonas's escape will cause the entire community great anguish for long periods of time until they have come to grips with the difficult memories he leaves behind him.

After his journey becomes difficult, the consequences of freedom become clearer to Jonas than they were in his memories or his meditations on choice and individuality. Feeling pain, hunger, and cold, Jonas realizes that all of his present misery is a direct result of his own actions. He understands for the first time that one choice always eliminates another choice. His community has chosen peace and comfort over extreme joy and pain, order over freedom, and Jonas sees that each choice has its advantages and disadvantages. But when he decides that the life he has chosen is better than the one he rejected, Jonas affirms that the important thing is choice. People with free choice have to accept the consequences of their actions, but in the end they will be happier to have the choice.

Jonas's powers of memory become undeniably magical on his journey. Earlier in the novel, the process of receiving memories has seemed mystical and mysterious, the opposite of the carefully reasoned, intricately explained rules of the community, symbolizing how removed the citizens are from the complexity of emotion. On the road, however, Jonas's mental powers become so strong that they are able to defy the community's sophisticated tracking technology and defeat the natural world. Memories of cold keep Jonas and Gabriel safe from the heat-seeking planes searching overhead, and memories of warmth help them to stay alive in the bitter cold. The extent of Jonas's powers to defy technology indicates that feelings have triumphed over cold logic in the story, regardless of whether Jonas survives his journey.

Jonas's deep loyalty to and affection for Gabriel also implies a triumph of the heart. Jonas has finally known love and the irrational, genuine sacrifices that we make to help someone we truly love.

When he risks his own life for Gabriel, and when hope for Gabriel's survival keeps him from giving up later in the journey, Jonas has achieved a love for another person that proves love is more than just pride or enjoyment.

When Jonas's supply of transmitted memories is exhausted, he turns instead to his own memories—of his parents, his friends, and the Giver. These memories can never fade, since they belong entirely to him. The hope that the memories give him shows that Jonas is truly beginning to live Elsewhere. He does not hold onto his personal memories out of practical necessity as the Elders hold onto memory in the form of the Giver. His memories exist simply to give his life meaning and pleasure, and to help him overcome personal obstacles. Love and choice both require memory, and Jonas loves, makes choices, and remembers.

The ending of *The Giver* is extremely ambiguous and highly controversial. It can be read in two ways: either Jonas and Gabriel have finally arrived at a populated section of Elsewhere—a place that holds on to the traditions that existed before Sameness, where they will be welcomed and loved—or they are both freezing to death, and in their delusion ecstatically imagine details from some of Jonas's stored memories. Some readers feel that the interpretation of the ending determines the message of the book. If the first interpretation is correct, the novel is optimistic, whereas the second one conveys a completely pessimistic and hopeless message. However, though the ambiguity provokes interesting questions and though the idea of Jonas and Gabriel freezing to death on the sled is a sad one, the message of the book remains optimistic no matter what has happened. In either case, Jonas is filled with real joy when he hears the music and sees the lights, and the story ends with Jonas and Gabriel full of hope, love, happiness, and uncertainty—all things that would never have been a part of their lives had they stayed in the community. When Jonas thinks over the choices he has made on his journey, he decides that "if he had stayed, he would have starved in other ways." A life full of choice, color, and emotion is more valuable to him than the alternative, no matter how long that life is. If Jonas does die at the end, he still dies only after having really lived. Note how at the end of the novel, Gabriel is referred to as a baby, not a newchild. Jonas and Gabriel are now both more human.

In either case, too, Jonas's escape from the community has sent his accumulated memories streaming back into the consciousness of the community. Whether or not he hears or imagines their singing behind him, Jonas knows that he has given them what he set out to give them: love and loneliness, freedom and choice. He has become the ultimate Giver of Memory, awakening his entire community to the possibilities of life. If the Christmastime village Jonas sees at the end of the novel does not really exist—if it is only a hallucination—we can still rest assured that in leaving his memories to the community, Jonas is turning his own community into that Christmas village. Enhanced by a new kind of sensory experience—music—that did not exist in Jonas's received memories, the village is as much a prophecy as it is a memory. The society is moving forward and looking back. The ending is undeniably hopeful.

IMPORTANT QUOTATIONS EXPLAINED

1. It was against the rules for children or adults to look at another's nakedness; but the rule did not apply to newchildren or the Old. Jonas was glad. . . . He couldn't see why it was necessary. He liked the feeling of safety here in this warm and quiet room; he liked the expression of trust on the woman's face as she lay in the water unprotected, exposed, and free.

In this quotation from Chapter 4, Jonas's mild exasperation with some of the community rules, combined with the "trust" and "safety" he feels while bathing the woman, subtly foreshadow the intense feelings of rebellion and the deep longing for love that accompany his training for Receiver. We see that,even before Jonas was exposed to the world of beauty, diversity, and emotion that the Giver opens up for him, he has some understanding of what is missing in his community, even though he still stays strictly within the rules.

Especially noteworthy is Jonas's use of the word "free": without her clothes, when she is "unprotected" and "exposed," the old woman is also free. Since her age and nakedness make her completely vulnerable to Jonas, it seems odd that Larissa could be described as free: any decision she makes can be easily vetoed, and any action she makes can be suppressed. Yet she is free of her clothes, and because of her age she is free of the social code that requires citizens to conceal their nakedness. For Jonas, this freedom from the social code is the most significant kind of freedom there is, and freedom from clothing becomes a metaphor for freedom from social conventions and rules. To be emotionally naked, for Jonas, is to dispense with the formalities of strict politeness and precise language. Jonas's use of the word "free" also reveals that he is already thinking about the limits his society puts on freedom.

The trust and safety he feels with the old woman also foreshadows his relationships with the Giver, an older man whom he begins to love like a grandfather, as well as his longing for a close relationship with grandparents. The description of the Christmas scene that teaches Jonas about grandparents evokes warmth and comfort in the same way that the scene with Larissa does, showing that Jonas is already sensitive to these pleasures.

2.   "We failed in our last selection," the Chief Elder said solemnly. "It was ten years ago, when Jonas was just a toddler. I will not dwell on the experience because it causes us all terrible discomfort."

This statement, made in Chapter 8 by the Chief Elder at the Ceremony of Twelve, when she introduces Jonas as the new Receiver, is the first reference anyone in *The Giver* makes to the first choice of Receiver, which failed ten years ago. Later in the novel, we learn that the discomfort the community suffered was the result of the many complicated, troubling memories that were released into everyone's minds after the failed Receiver-in-training, Rosemary, applied for release.

    The Chief Elder's description of the community's feelings as "discomfort" is telling. It indicates that the community is so unused to disturbance of any kind that even discomfort is such a traumatic experience that no one in the community ever wants to even mention it again. As we soon learn, it is forbidden to speak the name of the person who caused this discomfort (Jonas does not learn Rosemary's name until he asks the Giver.) At the same time, we realize that the community's seeming overreaction makes some sense, since the discomfort they felt was by far the worst suffering they had encountered in their lives. Discomfort is the strongest word available to them, given their emphasis on precise language.

    Rereading the Chief Elder's words later, in the context of Rosemary's actual experience—she was so traumatized by the memories she received that she applied for release—we realize that the word "discomfort" describes the community's inability to deal with the memories that flooded their minds, but it also reveals that the community does not grieve for the loss of Rosemary or regret the suffering that caused her suicide. As a substitute for the grief a community should feel, the phrase "discomfort" rings hollow.

3.   We really have to protect people from wrong choices.

Jonas speaks these words in Chapter 13, moments after having protested that he wished colors still existed so that people could have the pleasure and freedom of choosing between them. After some thought, his protests give way to the understanding that, if people were allowed to choose between colors, they might get so used to making choices that they would want to choose their jobs and their spouses. These are decisions that will have a serious effect on their lives and on the life of the community, and a wrong choice could be disastrous. In saying, "We really have to protect people from wrong choices," Jonas gives voice to the unspoken philosophy of benevolent oppression that pervades all aspects of life in the community. He has probably never thought of it this way before. Until this point, most references to the Committee of Elders emphasize the wise choices they make for the community but fail to mention that they are preventing individuals from making their own decisions. However, Jonas has been steeped in this philosophy all his life, and it comes out naturally when he tries to understand the structure of his own society. The very idea of "wrong choices" implies that Jonas has grown up believing that some choices *can* be objectively wrong. In a community as rigidly structured as his own, wrong choices exist: choices that can disrupt and damage the entire society. If the members of the community want the peace and order that the community provides, they must submit totally to the rules that keep the community running smoothly, and that means allowing other, more knowledgeable people to make choices for them.

However, in making this statement, Jonas has uncovered the negative aspect of the community's decision-making policies. In offering solutions to people who need them, the leaders of the community also prevent people from making their own choices. That this is done to protect them and that the choices are potentially wrong still cannot disguise the limitations imposed on the community members. These realizations bring Jonas a step closer to rebellion. Even as he says these words, he remains frustrated with the lack of color and choice in the community, and he begins to realize that his community's precise system of logic pales next to the wonders of his new experiences.

4.   "There's nothing we can do. It's always been this way.
     Before me, before you, before the ones who came before
     you. Back and back and back."

Jonas says this in Chapter 20 in an outburst of bitterness and
despair at the Giver's suggestion that the two of them might be able
to devise a plan to return the memories to the community. In saying
"back and back and back," he parrots a phrase used by the Giver in
early training sessions to explain the role of a Receiver within the
society. The phrase "back and back and back" is meant to express
the inevitability of the current situation: Sameness is not a historical
moment that has a beginning and an end, but an endless, changeless
state, something beyond time and space and human intervention.
The words have an incantatory quality, creating an atmosphere of
mystery around the origins of the community's traditions and conventions. This is an effective way to stifle revolution—if people do
not know that the status quo of society has ever been unstable or
uncertain, they cannot conceive of destabilizing it. This quality of
"back and back and back" is a major factor in the society's success.
No one thinks to question structures that are so ancient and
unchanging that they seem perfectly natural, and even though Jonas
and the Giver know that life existed before Sameness, they have no
memories of Sameness ever being defeated. In saying "back and
back and back" the Giver becomes complicit with the history-less,
memory-less community, resigning himself to a culture where nothing changes and the possibility of change is not acknowledged.

When Jonas takes the words "back and back and back" for his
own, he has assumed the world-weary, resigned attitude of the
Giver, abandoning his dreams of change for a hopeless, changeless
vision of the future. Since the words "back and back and back" con-
stitute an acceptance of the community's most important illusion—
that nothing has ever existed but Sameness—this moment could be
seen as a moment of defeat, in which Jonas feels utterly crushed by
the strict structures of the society. Luckily, however, the role reversal
is complete, and the Giver gains energy and hope even as Jonas
begins to despair.

5.   He heard people singing. Behind him, across vast distances
of space and time, from the place he had left, he thought he
heard music too. But perhaps it was only an echo.

These are the last lines of *The Giver*. The music that welcomes Jonas
to the Christmas-celebrating town is the first he has ever heard in his
life, and it signals not only his arrival in Elsewhere, where he can live
life to the fullest as he wants to, but also his awakening to a new kind
of perception, one that until this moment has been totally unavail-
able to him. This new sensory gift of music is a symbol of hope
and regeneration. Though he has left the Giver and his store of
memories, Jonas will experience countless exciting and terrifying
things in his new home, things that exist in the real world and not
just in memory. The singing also welcomes him to a new, different community. Here he will find human voices raised in beautiful music, ready to accept him and all of his differences and to
appreciate his beauty and love.

The origin of the music that Jonas hears behind him is as ambiguous as the ending of the novel itself. It could be the music that
Jonas's old community learns to make after the Giver helps them to
endure the memories that Jonas left behind him, an unmistakable
signal that their plan worked and worked well. At the same time, the
music may be merely an echo of the music playing in the town,
reminding Jonas that behind him his community is perhaps discov-
ering the delight of music at the same moment that he does. Alterna-
tively, both the music behind and in front of him could be figments
of his imagination, coming to him as he freezes to death with Gabriel on an empty hill. It could also simply represent Jonas's close link
to the Giver, who delights in music and wants to share most of his
pleasures with Jonas.

QUOTATIONS

KEY FACTS

FULL TITLE
The Giver

AUTHOR
Lois Lowry

TYPE OF WORK
Novel

GENRE
Young adult; science fiction; fantasy; dystopia

LANGUAGE
English

TIME AND PLACE WRITTEN
1993; United States

DATE OF FIRST PUBLICATION
1993

PUBLISHER
Houghton Mifflin

NARRATOR
The story is told by a third-person narrator whose point of view is limited to what Jonas observes and thinks.

POINT OF VIEW
The story is told completely from Jonas's point of view. We see all the actions and events through Jonas's eyes and do not have access to any information to which Jonas does not have access.

TONE
Lowry uses direct, simple language with very few figures of speech or ironic comments (though Jonas and the Giver make ironic statements.) The simplicity of the language is appropriate for Lowry's audience, children between eleven and fifteen, but it also echoes the "precision of language" demanded by Jonas's community. Despite the simplicity, the tone is somewhat elevated, suited to the nature of Jonas's discoveries about the richness of life.

TENSE
Past

SETTING (TIME)
An unspecified time in the future

SETTING (PLACE)
A utopian community that is part of a larger utopian society, presumably on Earth

PROTAGONIST
Jonas, an eleven-year-old boy who is chosen to be the new Receiver when he is twelve

MAJOR CONFLICT
Jonas's new emotional and sensory awareness cause him to rebel against the restrictions his society places on freedom of choice, individuality, emotion, and human experience.

RISING ACTION
When Jonas becomes the new Receiver, he receives memories that change the way he thinks about himself and his community forever.

CLIMAX
When Jonas realizes that when his father "releases" newchildren he actually kills them, Jonas reaches a point of no return. His frustration with his community and his desire to change it have been growing steadily, and finally Jonas cannot accept the society's insensitivity to the value of human life. He determines to change things.

FALLING ACTION
In order to put his plan into action, Jonas flees the community on bicycle with the newchild Gabe, evading search planes and enduring hunger and pain to try to bring feelings and color to his community and bring himself to the world he has dreamed of knowing.

THEMES
The importance of memory; the relationship between pain and pleasure; the importance of the individual

MOTIFS
Vision; nakedness; release

SYMBOLS
The newchild Gabriel; the sled; the river

FORESHADOWING
Important examples of foreshadowing in *The Giver* include Jonas's apprehension about the Ceremony of Twelve, which foreshadows his future disillusionment with the community; and his feeling of closeness and freedom with the old woman while he bathes her, which foreshadows his longing for grandparents and other close, personal connections.

Study Questions & Essay Topics

Study Questions

1. *The ending of* THE GIVER *has been interpreted in a few different ways. Choose one possible interpretation of the ending and argue its validity, using clues from the text to explain your conclusions.*

The two major interpretations of *The Giver*'s ending are that (1) Jonas and Gabriel have truly escaped the physical boundaries of their society and discovered a real village in Elsewhere, and (2) Jonas's vision of the village is only a hallucination that he experiences as he and Gabriel freeze to death in the snow in the middle of nowhere. Both arguments can be solidly supported by references in the text.

In order to argue that the two children freeze to death in the snow and that their vision of the village is only an illusion, we can rely on the uncanny similarity between the landscape Jonas sees—or thinks he sees—and the memories the Giver has transmitted to him in the past. It is extremely unlikely that Jonas would come upon a hill that looks just like the hill from his memory of the ride on the sled, and then come upon an identical sled waiting to take him to the bottom of the hill. Given that for the last leg of their journey, Jonas has been relying on memories of sunshine to keep himself and Gabriel alive and happy, it would make sense that Jonas relies on the most pleasant memories he has when the cold and exhaustion grow too much for them. When Jonas admits that the music he thinks he hears behind him might be "only an echo," he could be implying that the vision before him is an echo too—of his own memory. Another point to consider is that it seems unlikely that Jonas could travel on a bicycle further than search planes could fly and that communities that have not gone over to Sameness could be found so (relatively) close to Jonas's own community.

To argue that Jonas and Gabriel do survive and reach the village safely to begin a new life, we can explain that although the events of the last pages mirror events from Jonas's memories, we learn toward the end of the book that Jonas is losing all of the memories that were transmitted to him by the Giver. The last memory that brings him joy is not a memory of sunshine, but a "real" memory of people Jonas has met in his life—his friends and family. This suggests that the things Jonas sees in the world around him are really there, since he has lost the memories. The music that he hears is real, because music was never a part of his memory. The serendipitous appearance of the sled is strange, but not inconsistent with the atmosphere of magic and mysticism that pervades Jonas's new life and his relationship with the Giver.

2. *Among other things, the community in* THE GIVER
    *eliminates most traditional distinctions between men
    and women, but occasionally stereotypes and customs
    still exist to distinguish male children from female
    children and men from women. What rules remain in
    place in the community that differentiate men from
    women? Why do you think these specific rules were
    retained while others were not?*

Even though Lowry seems to take pains to eliminate gender stereotypes in the society in *The Giver*, supporting the idea that everyone in the society is as similar to one another as possible, ideas about the differences between men and women still linger. Of course, it makes sense that girls are given "special undergarments" at age eleven, but it makes less sense that girls wear braids with hair ribbons until age nine. The hair ribbons are the only decorative element mentioned in the entire novel. Perhaps they are just used to distinguish girls from boys, ignoring the original, aesthetic purpose of hair ribbons. Another vestige of gender roles is the structure of the family units: though the roles of "mother" and "father" are not clearly defined, each family consists of a father, mother, sister, and brother. Since no one has sex, and the parents do not produce children together, the persistence of heterosexual couples is either a meaningless echo of the traditional nuclear family or an effort to provide both male and female children with appropriate role models. In any case, the community seems to appropriate some of the gender distinctions of pre-Sameness society, but uses them for entirely different purposes.

The Giver, however, seems to have more nostalgic, traditional notions about gender differences, or at least about femininity. His description of Rosemary emphasizes traditionally feminine qualities: she is beautiful, delicate, and sensitive. He has trouble giving her memories of physical pain and suffering, although he gives them much more easily to Jonas. Jonas, too, associates femininity with gentleness and fragility, even though his father is clearly more gentle and nurturing than his mother. When the Giver tells him about Rosemary, Jonas thinks that he would never want his "favorite female" Fiona to suffer as he has suffered, enduring the difficult memories. Perhaps the nostalgia that the Giver and Jonas feel toward the pre-Sameness period extends to the pre-Sameness traditions of gender differences.

3. *In a book like* THE GIVER, *which features a society unlike our own, to whom some concepts we consider ordinary would seem completely outlandish, the author must present familiar things—sleds, love, sunburns—with fresh eyes. Choose something ordinary that is described as extraordinary in the book, and evaluate Lowry's success in capturing strangers' reactions to the familiar object.*

One of the first moments when Jonas encounters something familiar to us, the readers, but totally unfamiliar to him is the moment when the apple changes in midair. Not only is the moment significant as the first time we see Jonas experience something totally new, but it presents an interesting challenge to both the reader and the writer: at this early point in the story, Jonas has not yet begun his training, and so he does not expect unusual things to happen to him. When the apple changes, Lowry must communicate the quality of its change without using any vocabulary or ideas that Jonas would not already know. She cannot tell us directly that there is no color in Jonas's world, since the entire story is told from Jonas's perspective: he does not know what color is, so he does not know that color exists. Lowry has to show us somehow that something is missing from Jonas's world, so that we recognize the "change" that Jonas witnesses as the restoration of the missing quality.

To accomplish this, Lowry places subtle clues throughout the story that call attention to the absence of color. When Lily describes the newchild's eyes, for example, she mentions that they are "funny" like Jonas's, without making any mention of their color.

Jonas's meditation about his own eyes continues for a long time without any mention of their color, only of their shade, something that might strike us as slightly unusual. When Jonas takes note of all of the physical qualities of the apple after he has seen it briefly change, he mentions size, shape, and shade, but never the color. This clue is extremely subtle, since "shade" can be a synonym for "color." The discordant element here is Jonas's statement that the shade of the apple is "nondescript" like his tunic: we assume the apple is red, and few people would call red "nondescript." In using subtle indications like these, Lowry allows us to participate in Jonas's bewilderment at the apple's change—we stretch our imaginations wondering how an apple could change—and at the same time prepares us for the Giver's revelation that Jonas is beginning to see color.

SUGGESTED ESSAY TOPICS

1. One of the more controversial topics that Lowry touches upon in THE GIVER is euthanasia, or the practice of ending someone's life to ease their suffering. Jonas's community practices euthanasia on very old citizens as well as upon unhealthy newchildren. Jonas's horror at this practice motivates him to take drastic measures to reform the society, and yet many people in our own society consider euthanasia to be a compassionate practice and one that should be available to all citizens. Discuss the attitude toward euthanasia as expressed in THE GIVER. Does the novel condemn, promote, or conditionally accept the practice?

2. It is difficult for us to imagine a world without color, personal freedoms, and love, but in THE GIVER, the society relinquishes these things in order to make room for total peace and safety. Consider the pleasures and experiences that our own society discourages in order to preserve the public good (certain recreational drugs, for example.) In the context of the lessons Jonas learns in THE GIVER, explain why we should or should not sacrifice an orderly community in order to allow individuals more spiritually or sensually satisfying experiences. Where do you think the line between public safety and personal freedom should be drawn?

3. Read at least one other novel depicting a dystopian society. What techniques does this society use to maintain order? How does its structure differ from the community's in THE GIVER?

4. Consider the community's repression of sexuality in THE GIVER. What function does it serve in helping the society run smoothly? What dangers does sexuality pose to a structured community, and how are those dangers different from the dangers posed by love? If you have read BRAVE NEW WORLD by Aldous Huxley, compare that society's use of sexuality and promiscuity to keep people from accessing deeper feelings to

THE GIVER's *restriction of sexuality for essentially the same ends.*

5. *Despite the community's emphasis on precise language, language is often used as a tool for social control in* THE GIVER. *Choose two or three words used in the society (examples are release, newchild, Stirrings) that distort or conceal the meaning of the words we use now in order to promote the rules and conventions of the community, and describe how their use affects the behavior and attitudes of the people in the community.*

6. THE GIVER *is one of the most frequently censored books in America, partially because some critics believe that Lowry is promoting the community Jonas lives in as an exemplary place to live. Although it might be extreme to suppose that Lowry supports all of the institutions that her protagonist rejects, examine* THE GIVER's *attitude toward the community rules and culture. Which aspects of the community are the targets of the most criticism and condemnation? Do any aspects of the society escape criticism?*

7. *Analyze* THE GIVER's *relationship to the social questions that were most frequently discussed in the early 1990s. To what degree is* THE GIVER *a cautionary tale? Who is the object of its warning?*

Review & Resources

Quiz

1. In the first chapter, why is the Pilot released from the community?

    A. He was a spy from an enemy community
    B. He failed to deliver his cargo of food on time
    C. He misread his navigational instructions and frightened the community
    D. He crashed his aircraft

2. Why does Jonas decide that "apprehensive" is a better word for his feeling than "frightened"?

    A. He wants to use more sophisticated vocabulary, since he is turning twelve soon
    B. He thinks it expresses more precisely how he feels
    C. He likes words that begin with vowels
    D. His mother once used the word "apprehensive" and he admires her

3. What does Jonas's mother do for a living?

    A. She is a Nurturer
    B. She is a Storyteller
    C. She is a Birthmother
    D. She works for the department of justice

4. Which rule is most frequently broken in Jonas's community?

    A. Children must not ride bicycles until they are nine
    B. Adults and children are not allowed to look at each other naked
    C. Aircrafts are not to be flown over the community
    D. The names of newchildren are secret until the Naming Ceremony

5. Why does Jonas's mother discourage Lily from becoming a Birthmother?

    A. Giving birth is dangerous, and Lily might die from the complications

    B. Birthmothers are very lazy and never get anything done

    C. The position holds very little honor in the society

    D. The society is overpopulated

6. Why does Jonas worry about Asher's Assignment?

    A. Asher is easily disappointed and will probably find fault with his assignment

    B. Asher does not seem to have any serious interests

    C. Asher will fail at any Assignment he is given

    D. Asher has not completed enough volunteer hours to qualify for an Assignment

7. Why is Gabriel in danger of being released?

    A. He bites the staff at the Nurturing Center

    B. He is deformed

    C. He is not growing fast enough and cannot sleep through the night

    D. He smiles too much, and the staff suspects he will be abnormally gassy when he grows up

8. What do the numbers assigned to each child signify?

    A. The order of their birth

    B. Their rank in school

    C. The department to which they belong

    D. Their height in inches

9. Why does the Chief Elder apologize to the audience at the Ceremony of Twelve?

    A. She is about to tell them that Jonas will be released

    B. She has caused them anxiety about Jonas's Assignment

    C. Her shoes do not match her handbag

    D. She knows they are disappointed with their children's Assignments

REVIEW & RESOURCES

10. How does the community react to the death of a child in the river?

   A. They hold a candlelight vigil
   B. They send casseroles to the child's parents
   C. They hold seminars to warn children to stay away from the river
   D. They chant the child's name over and over, each time more and more softly

11. Where did the Giver get his wisdom?

   A. From his own experience
   B. From reading books
   C. From memories transmitted by the previous Receiver
   D. From a surgical operation

12. Which of the following was *not* written on Jonas's Assignment sheet?

   A. You are permitted to lie
   B. You are not permitted to apply for release
   C. You are not permitted to apply for a spouse
   D. You are exempted from rules governing rudeness

13. What method does the Giver use to train Jonas?

   A. He places his hands on Jonas's bare back and gives him memories
   B. He burns Jonas with a hot iron repeatedly until Jonas can endure pain
   C. He teaches Jonas to read novels with a critical eye
   D. He shows Jonas videos of events that happened in the distant past

14. What are Stirrings?

   A. Leftover pancake batter
   B. Intense religious gatherings at which members of the community vent their suppressed emotions
   C. The feelings that usher in the first time someone can see color
   D. The beginnings of sexual desire

15. What is the first memory Jonas receives?

    A. A ride on a sled through falling snow
    B. A sunburn
    C. A family at Christmas
    D. A ride on a sled resulting in a broken leg

16. Why is Lily skeptical of Jonas's story about the elephants?

    A. She is afraid of elephants, so she thinks Jonas is just trying to scare her
    B. Jonas is a pathological liar
    C. Lily has been raised to think that elephants are imaginary creatures
    D. Lily is an expert on elephants and knows they would never behave in the way Jonas describes them

17. What was the name of the failed Receiver who was chosen ten years ago?

    A. Poppy
    B. Melanie
    C. Fiona
    D. Rosemary

18. Why is Jonas not permitted to apply for release?

    A. If Jonas left the community, all the valuable time and money spent on his training would be wasted
    B. If Jonas left the community, all of the Committee of Elders would die of broken hearts because they love him so much
    C. If Jonas left the community, all the memories he had accumulated would enter the minds of the citizens and create chaos
    D. If Jonas left, the Giver would be lonely

19. How does Jonas help the newchild Gabriel go to sleep?

    A. He transmits memories of lullabies and soft beds
    B. He tells him bedtime stories
    C. He transmits memories of peaceful sails on a lake
    D. He injects him with a mild sleeping drug

20. Why do Jonas's parents refuse to tell him that they love him?

    A.   They think that Jonas will feel smothered by their love

    B.   They secretly hate him

    C.   They think love is an obsolete word with no meaning

    D.   They were not paying attention when he asked if they loved him

21. Why does Jonas interrupt his friends' game of good guys and bad guys?

    A.   They did not let him play

    B.   They are not following the rules governing gameplay

    C.   He has a better idea for a game and thinks his rank as Receiver should count for something

    D.   He recognizes that their game takes a casual attitude toward tragedy

22. Why does the Nurturing Center release one of every set of identical twins?

    A.   The staff is sadistic

    B.   It is inconvenient to have identical people walking around

    C.   They need to practice their releasing techniques

    D.   One twin is always seriously ill at birth

23. Why does Jonas leave the community before the time he and the Giver had planned?

    A.   He realizes that the Giver is conspiring with the Committee of Elders to trap him

    B.   He finds out that Gabriel will be released the next morning and wants to save his life

    C.   The wind is good, and he needs to take a boat

    D.   He wants to bring Fiona, and he knows the Giver would not approve

24. How does Jonas keep the search planes from finding him and Gabriel?

   A. He covers their bodies with thick, dirty leaves
   B. He bribes one of the Pilots to ignore them
   C. He transmits memories of cold so that the heat-seeking planes cannot locate them
   D. He stays very still because they are motion-sensitive

25. What does Jonas see (or think he sees) as he nears the bottom of the hill on the sled?

   A. Colored lights in the windows of houses
   B. His parents waiting for him
   C. A search party from the community
   D. A child with a broken leg who has fallen from his sled

ANSWER KEY:

1: C; 2: B; 3: D; 4: A; 5: C; 6: B; 7: C; 8: A; 9: B; 10: D; 11:
C; 12: C; 13: A; 14: D; 15: A; 16: C; 17: D; 18: C; 19: C; 20:
C; 21: D; 22: B; 23: B; 24: C; 25: A

SUGGESTIONS FOR FURTHER READING

CHRISTOPHER, JOHN. *The Guardians*. New York: Macmillan, 1970.

HUXLEY, ALDOUS. *Brave New World*. New York: Harper Perennial, 1998.

MENEXAS, VICKY. "Efferent and Aesthetic Stance: Understanding the Definition of Lois Lowry's THE GIVER as Metaphor." *Journal of Children's Literature*, 23(2): p34–41, Fall 1997.

ORWELL, GEORGE. *1984*. New York: Knopf, 1982.

SMITH, AMANDA. "PW Interviews: Lois Lowry." *Publishers Weekly*, 152–153, 21 February 1986.

TROSKY, SUSAN M., ed. "Lowry, Lois." *Contemporary Authors*. Detroit: Gale Research, 1994.

ZAIDMAN, LAURA M. "Lois Lowry." *Dictionary of Literary Biography*. Ed. Glenn E. Estes. Detroit: Gale Research, 1986.

REVIEW & RESOURCES